# THE
# TRANSITION
## BETWEEN
# TWO
# COVENANTS

Published by:
JaDon Management Inc.
1405 4th Ave. N. W. #109
Ardmore, Ok. 73401


Cover Design by
Jeffrey T. McCormack
The Pendragon: Web and Graphic Design
www.the pendragon.net

# DEDICATED:

**To all who do and who will choose the scriptures over tradition and engage in the battle to reform biblical eschatology, thank you.**

# FOREWORD

As a young man, the fellowship in which I was raised taught as a basic, undeniable (and unchallengeable) doctrine, that the Law of Moses was nailed to the cross. God was supposedly through with Old Covenant Israel at the cross. I believed and taught that idea. The idea of a transitional period of time for the changing of the covenants was a foreign idea.

As a result of that early "training" I foolishly believed that one could understand eschatology independently of an understanding of the end of the Old Covenant (the Law of Moses) and the full arrival of the New Covenant of Christ.

Thankfully, in the ensuing years, with more study and more careful consideration, I came to realize how *badly mistaken* I had been in those younger days. I well remember the shock, I can almost call it the trauma, of discovering how important covenantal transition was and is to the eschatological narrative. I came to realize that the transition of the covenants was and is inseparably tied to, and even to be identified with, *resurrection*!

The transition from the Mosaic Covenant, that Paul called "The ministration of death" to the New Covenant of Christ is, in fact, fundamental and critical for a proper understanding of the doctrine of last days, the coming of the Lord, the judgment and the resurrection.

What I would have given in those younger years to have a resource like what you hold in your hands! The simplicity, the compelling logic, the careful exegetic argumentation that Dan Dery presents in this work would have saved me a lot of struggle, a lot of time!

If you have thought- as I did - that God was through with the Old Covenant, and with Old Covenant Israel, at the Cross, I urge you to read this book carefully with Bible in hand. You will be amazed at how clear, how powerful, how convincing and compelling Dery's careful exegesis is! If you have questions about when the Old Covenant passed away, this book will provide you solid, Biblical answers.

Some of the topics developed by Dery are: The Inheritance Through Covenant Transition, The Kingdom through Covenant Transition, and Restoring the Image of God Through Covenant Transition. These three chapters are my favorites. I think they will become your's as well.

I am persuaded that after reading this short, but power packed book, that you will agree with me, that it is a "must read" for understanding the Transition of the Two Covenants - and for understanding the Biblical story of eschatology. It is simply *a good book!*

Don K. Preston (D. Div.)
President and Founder - Preterist Research Institute
Ardmore, Ok. 73401
www.eschatology.org

# WORD FROM THE AUTHOR

I would like to express my sincere appreciation that you have taken the time to begin reading this book. There are many things to do in this life, and time is limited, so I am truly grateful for the sacrifice of your time.

I would also like to specifically thank Dr. Don K. Preston, Dr. William Bell, Dr. Lynn Hiles, and Danny Ray Phillips, as teachers of God's word from whom I have had the privilege of learning from, either directly or indirectly. This book would not exist without you and your desire to know and to teach truth. Thank you.

Most importantly, I am grateful for my Lord and Savior Jesus Christ. It is my greatest privilege that I can know Him, and draw ever closer to Him. My desire in life is that I may learn and know His truth, and be courageous enough to follow His truth wherever it leads.

This book is about the present total victory over sin and death in Jesus Christ. It is about believing and receiving the gospel of the kingdom. It is about embracing the New Covenant and all its present redemptive and covenantal blessings in Christ. It is about the consummated redemptive work of Christ which His Body received nearly 2000 years ago. This book is about consummated restoration through covenantal transition.

What follows will challenge some modern traditions and beliefs, but I encourage the reader to search the scriptures and see if these things are so, this is noble in the sight of the Lord.

The purpose of this book is to bring the glory and honor due to the Lord Jesus by the proclamation of His present consummated redemptive work in and through His New Covenant. It is my conviction that today, through the New Covenant, man has been fully restored and redeemed to God through the redemptive work of Christ, and because His work is finished, we now dwell in the presence of God, in the image of God.

May the Lord bless you as you carefully read and study this book, and may the good news of the finished work of Jesus fill your heart and mind as you walk with him.

Let us begin explore together the transition between two covenants.

# TABLE OF CONTENTS

## CHAPTER 1:
## ESTABLISHING THE FIRST CENTURY COVENANTAL TRANSITION

## CHAPTER 2:
## THE INHERITANCE THROUGH COVENANTAL TRANSITION

## CHAPTER 3:
## THE KINGDOM THROUGH COVENANTAL TRANSITION

# CHAPTER 4:
# THE IMAGE OF GOD RESTORED THROUGH COVENANTAL TRANSITION

# CHAPTER 5:

# CHAPTER
# ONE

## ESTABLISHING A FIRST CENTURY
## COVENANTAL TRANSITION

Let us begin with what I believe to be a fundamental interpretive paradigm for the New Testament. It is my opinion that if one fails to understand this paradigm, he is doomed to error in the study of eschatology and destined for mass confusion and contradiction in his overall system of theology. I will also say this, if this paradigm can be demonstrated to be untrue according to the scriptures, my entire system of eschatology and theology crumbles to the ground. Here is the paradigm:

> **Between AD30 and AD 70 there was a forty-year covenantal transition taking place. Said another way, for forty years beginning at the cross, the Old Covenant began "vanishing away" and the New Covenant was being established.**

Now granted, if someone would have told me this several years ago, I would have looked at them as if they had lost their mind. I literally would not have had the foggiest idea about what they would have meant. After all, wasn't the Old Covenant fulfilled at the cross and nailed to it? Isn't that what Jesus meant when he said, "it is finished"? Didn't the tearing of the veil of the temple symbolize this? And what about the New Covenant? Wasn't the New Covenant fully established and all its blessings fully received at the cross?

The answers to these questions was not what I expected.

To say that many commentators, teachers, and preachers would answer these questions in the affirmative is a huge understatement. The idea that the Old Covenant was fulfilled and the New Covenant was fully established at the cross as an instantaneous event, is all but "common knowledge" among many modern Christians. But is this majority view the biblical view? Or, do the scriptures tell a radically different story concerning the covenants?

## JESUS MADE THE GOLDEN RULE

**Think not that I have come to abolish the law and the prophets, I have not come to abolish them but to fulfil them. For truly, I say to you, till heaven and earth pass away, not an iota, not a dot, will pass from the law until all is accomplished**
(Mathew 5:17-18 RSV)

Without getting into an in-depth study of this verse (see Don Preston's book From Torah to Telos volume 1 for an exhaustive study of that text), why don't we just take it at face value. To do that, let's look at it from two perspectives.

1. …. till heaven and earth pass away, not an iota, not a dot, will pass from the law…

From this perspective, none of the Law could or would pass away (become covenantally obsolete), until heaven and earth passed away. This is a powerful truth, and enough to give any futurist eschatology serious problems, but the second perspective is the one we will focus on.

> 2. …. not an iota, not a dot, will pass from the law until all is accomplished

The word "accomplished" is the Greek word "*ginomai*" and means "to become, to come into existence, to come to pass". From this perspective, Jesus is saying that until all the Law came to pass / came into existence, none of the Law could or would pass away.

There is no getting around the words of Jesus, they are clear and unambiguous. No Old Testament prophecy (and by implication, the entire Old Covenant) could or would pass away until everything of which it prophesied had been fulfilled (come into existence). It is in these words of Jesus that we can understand, at least on one level, the necessity for the post-cross covenantal transition.

> **It was during this forty year period that all prophecy contained in the Law and the Prophets was being fully accomplished. It was coming into existence through fulfillment.**

# THE APOSTLES PREACHED THE GOLDEN RULE

Now, if it's like much of the "Church world" says, that the entire Old Covenant was fulfilled and abolished at the cross, then we should expect the New Testament writers to trumpet that message. However, rather than teaching that the Law was fulfilled and the Old Covenant abolished at the cross, they proclaim with a most unified voice, decades after the cross, that their hope (and the hope of all Israel) was nothing but the fulfillment of the Old Covenant Law and prophets.

As faithful disciples, the apostles of Jesus preached the gospel according to the golden rule established by their master.

## PETER'S MESSAGE

**Blessed be the God and Father of our Lord Jesus Christ. According to his great mercy, he has caused us to be born again to a living hope through the resurrection of Jesus Christ from the dead, to an inheritance that is imperishable, undefiled, and unfading, kept in heaven for you. Who by God's power are being guarded through faith for a salvation ready to be revealed in the last time…. Concerning this salvation, the**

prophets who prophesied about the grace that was to be yours searched and inquired carefully, inquiring what person or time the Spirit of Christ in them was indicating when he predicted the sufferings of Christ and the subsequent glories. It was revealed to them that they were serving not themselves but you, in the things that have now been announced to you through those who preached the good news…. Therefore, prepare your minds for action, and being sober minded, set your hope fully on the grace that will be brought to you at the revelation of Jesus Christ. (1 Peter 1:3-13 ESV)

Peter said that their hope in the salvation that was "ready to be revealed" was the inheritance that the Old Testament prophets said would come to them. In other words, the salvation-inheritance they were hoping for would be the fulfillment of Old Testament prophecy.

For He must remain in heaven until the time for the final restoration of all things, as God promised long ago through his holy prophets. Moses said, "The Lord your God will raise up for you a prophet like me from among your own people". Listen carefully to everything he tells you. Then Moses said, "Anyone who will not listen to that prophet will be completely cut off

**from God's people"**. **Starting with Samuel, every prophet spoke about what is happening today.** (Acts 3:20-24 (NLT)

Peter said that what was happening in his days (which was after the cross) was in fulfillment of what the Old Covenant prophets had foretold (Joel 2, Isaiah 32, Ezekiel 37 etc.) Also, the final restoration of all things (which had already begun through the ministry of John the Baptist) would be the fulfillment of the promises of God which were spoken by the prophets and found in the Old Testament scriptures.

> **For Peter, the pouring out of the eschatological Spirit was the evidence that the Messianic restoration in fulfillment of the prophets had begun and would soon be consummated.**

**This is now the second letter that I am writing to you, beloved. In both of them I am stirring up your sincere mind by way of reminder, that you should remember the predictions of the holy prophets…. They will say, "where is the promise of his coming…." The Lord is not slow to fulfill his promise as some count slowness…. But according to his promise we are waiting for a new heavens and a new earth in which righteousness dwells.** (2 Peter 3:1-13 ESV)

Peter once again says that the Lord's "coming" (Parousia) as well as the new heaven and new earth was a promise of the Lord and prediction (prophesy) of the holy (Old Testament) prophets. For Peter, his eschatological hope was the fulfillment of the Old Covenant prophesies found in the Law and the prophets. Therefore, according to the apostle to the circumcision, not only were the Law and the prophets (the Old Covenant), not fulfilled at the cross, they would not be fulfilled until the bringing in of the new heavens and new earth and the "restoration of all things".

## JOHN'S MESSAGE

**And the angel who I saw standing on the sea and on the land raised his right hand to heaven and swore by him who lives forever and ever…. that there would be no more delay, but in the days of the trumpet call to be sounded by the seventh angel, the mystery of God would be fulfilled, just as he announced to his servants the prophets. (Revelation 10:5-7)**

More than thirty years after the cross, the apostle of love tells us that the fulfillment of the "mystery of God" (God's redemptive plan-Ephesians 3:1-11) would be the fulfillment of what the Old Covenant prophets announced. Clearly, the apostle John did not see the Law and the prophets as "fully accomplished" (fulfilled) at the cross.

Notice also that in verses 5-6 of Revelation 10, John quotes

Daniel 12:7 nearly verbatim. Daniel saw the angel **"standing on the sea and on the land raised his right hand to heaven and swore by him who lives forever and ever"**. This implies that it is specifically the resurrection at the "time of the end" of Daniel 12 that John interprets in Revelation 10 as "the mystery of God" (Jew and Gentile raised up in one body), as explained in Ephesians 2-4.

This means that the "mystery of God" (the "perfected" body of Christ was the "hope of Israel" (the resurrection - Acts 28:20). The implications of this are profound indeed.

# PAUL'S MESSAGE

Although the Apostle Paul was not with Peter and John when Jesus laid down the golden rule in Mathew 5:17-18, he apparently still got the memo.

> **Brothers, I am a Pharisee, as were my ancestors. And I am on trial because my hope is in the resurrection of the dead.**
> (Acts 23:6 NLT)

> **But I admit that I follow the Way, which they call a cult. I worship the God of our ancestors, and I firmly believe the Jewish law and everything written in the prophets. I have the same hope**

**in God that these men have, that he will raise
both the righteous and the unrighteous.**
(Acts 24:14-15 NLT)

Paul's hope was the resurrection of the righteous and the
unrighteous, but, his hope was based on the "Jewish Law and
everything written in the prophets". In other words, Paul's
eschatological resurrection hope was the fulfillment (the full
accomplishment) of the Old Testament Law and prophets.

> **Now I am on trial because of my hope in the
> fulfillment of God's promise made to our
> ancestors. In fact, that is why the twelve tribes
> of Israel zealously worship God day and night,
> and they share the same hope I have…. Why
> does it seem incredible that God can raise the
> dead…But God has protected me right up to this
> present time so I can testify to everyone, from
> the least to the greatest. I teach nothing except
> what the prophets and Moses said would
> happen. That the Messiah would suffer and be
> the first to rise from the dead, and in this way
> announce God's light to Jews and Gentiles alike.**
> (Acts 26:6-23 NLT)

Paul says that his resurrection hope was the same hope that the
Jews (all 12 tribes of Israel) were at that time anticipating, and
this hope would be the fulfillment of the promise that God made
to their fathers, recorded in their Old Testament scriptures. As

Paul sums it up, his resurrection hope - as a Jewish Christian - was the "hope of Israel", which was the "one hope of his calling" (Ephesians 4:4)

> **For this reason therefore, I have asked to see and speak with you, since it is because of the hope of Israel that I am wearing this chain.**
> (Acts 28:20 ESV)

Then in his famous resurrection discourse, Paul says….

> **When the perishable puts on imperishable, and the mortal puts on immortality, then shall come to pass the saying that is written "Death is swallowed up in victory". O death, where is your sting"** (1 Corinthians 15:54-55)

For the great apostle to the gentiles, his hope in the final consummative resurrection was the hope of Israel which he anticipated as the fulfillment of what was written in the Law and the prophets (Isaiah 25:8, Hosea 13:14).

As we have seen above, Peter, John, and Paul, all taught decades after the cross that their eschatological hope was still the promises that God made to their fathers in fulfillment and accomplishment of the Old Testament Law and prophets. This is irrefutable proof that the Law and the prophets (the entire Old Testament and the Old Covenant contained therein) had not been fulfilled nor abolished at the cross as modern mainstream Christianity teaches.

11

On the contrary, the unified and consistent apostolic testimony was that all Old Testament prophecy would not be fulfilled until the time of the consummative restoration of all things, that is, the time of the resurrection and the salvation-inheritance of Israel.

> **The simple reality is that it's impossible to logically say that the Old Covenant (the Law and prophets) was fulfilled at the cross, and at the same time say that you are still hoping for the resurrection, which Paul said, would be the fulfillment of the law and prophets.**

This is more than a major problem for all futurist paradigms, it's an insurmountable biblical contradiction which will profoundly impact all who desire truth over tradition. It was the simple yet powerful teaching that Jesus had established decades prior, to which his disciples clung tenaciously throughout their proclamation of the gospel....

>**"... not an iota, not a dot, will pass from the law until all is accomplished".**

And so, we have demonstrated from the scriptures that the inspired apostolic testimony was that decades after the cross the Law and the prophets had still not been fulfilled/accomplished. This was according to Jesus' words in Mathew 5:17-18 that none of the Law could/would pass until all of the Law was fulfilled.

Therefore, between AD30 and AD 70, the Old Covenant remained unfulfilled and unabolished, and as we shall see, both New and Old Covenants were in the process of covenantal transition.

## PRIESTHOOD GUARANTEES COVENANT

Having established that the Old Covenant was not fulfilled and abolished at the cross, we can now begin to demonstrate that the scriptures teach a first century "covenantal transition". As we have already alluded to:

> **The purpose of this transitional period was to fulfill (fully accomplish) the Law and the prophets (the entire Old Covenant) which would bring God's redemptive purpose and man's redemptive destiny to completion.**

In Hebrews chapter 5 the writer establishes the fact that Jesus had been made a high priest, not after the order of the sons of Levi under the Old Covenant, but after a new and better order, one that was necessary to establish a New and better Covenant.

**"So also Christ did not exalt himself to be made a high priest, but was appointed by him who said to him "You are my Son, today I have begotten you". As he says also in another place "You are a priest forever, after the order of Melchizedek"** (Hebrews 5:5-6 ESV)

Then in Hebrews 6, the writer demonstrates that as God showed Abraham the unchanging nature of his promise by an oath, he has likewise, yet even "more convincingly" shown the heirs of the promise (the first century generation of saints) the unchanging character of his purpose by guaranteeing Christ's high-priesthood with an oath. In other words, it was because of the high-priesthood-oath made to Christ that the Hebrews were being encouraged to take hold of the promise made to their father Abraham as the "hope set before them".

**"For when God made a promise to Abraham, since he had no one greater by whom to swear, he swore by himself, saying "Surely I will bless you and multiply you". And thus Abraham, having patiently waited, obtained the promise. For people swear by something greater than themselves, and in all their disputes an oath is final for confirmation". So, when God who desired to show more convincingly to the heirs of the promise the unchangeable character of his purpose, he guaranteed it with an oath, that**

**by two unchangeable things, in which it is impossible for God to lie, we who have fled for refuge might have strong encouragement to hold fast to the hope set before us".**

(Hebrews 6:13-18 ESV)

In chapter 7 the writer explains the reason for the need of a high priest after the order of Melchizedek... because the former priesthood could not bring to perfection their hope, that is, the promise made to Abraham. Under the Levitical priesthood, the people "received the Law", and therefore it was that priesthood which ministered the Law yet could never minister righteousness. (Galatians 3:21)

> **"Now if perfection had been attainable through the Levitical priesthood (for under it the people received the Law), what further need would there have been for another priest to arise after the order of Melchizedek, rather than one named after the order of Aaron?**
> (Hebrews 7:11 ESV)

So, in order to bring in "New Covenant perfection" (Hebrews 6:1f), the priesthood was at that time "being changed" ("changed" is in the present tense in verse 12). And since the priesthood administers and perpetuates the covenant (and therefore guarantees covenant), it was necessary that the Law (covenant) be changed with the priesthood.

**"For when there is a change in the priesthood, there is necessarily a change in the law as well"** (Hebrews 7:12 ESV)

Next, the writer sums up the significance of the fact that a new priesthood had been established and what it meant concerning the New Covenant.

**"For on the one hand, a former commandment is set aside because of its weakness and uselessness (for the law made nothing perfect)"** (Hebrews 7:18-19 ESV)

The "former commandment" (which was literally "being set aside" – present tense) was specifically the commandment concerning the genealogical requirement of the Levitical priesthood, which was a commandment under the Old Law. It was the commandment concerning priesthood that administered, guaranteed and perpetuated the Old Covenant and gave "hope" to Israel concerning the promise to Abraham. However, the fact that the Levitical priesthood could not consummate and "perfect" that hope, made the commandment (and the entire Old Covenant) weak and useless, and was therefore "being set aside". Notice what the writer of Hebrews says next....

**"….. but on the other hand, a better hope is introduced, through which we draw near to God. And it was not without an oath. For**

**these who formerly became priests were made such without an oath, but this one was made a priest with an oath by the one who said to him "You are a priest forever".** (Hebrews 7:19-21 ESV)

The better hope introduced was "that which was not without an oath". What was it that was "not without an oath"? It was the making of Jesus the high priest (it was **with an oath**-verse 21).

---

In other words, the fact that Jesus was made high priest with an oath after the order of Melchizedek, was the introducing of a "better hope" – for Israel.

---

Therefore, the Old Covenant hope of Israel which was based on the weak and useless commandment concerning the Levitical priesthood (which although guaranteed and maintained the Old Covenant, could never bring the promises of that covenant to perfection), was being set aside for "the better hope". This better hope was based upon the oath of Christ's Melchizedekian priesthood which guaranteed the consummation of the New Covenant, through the perfection and fulfillment of the promises under the old.

**"This makes Jesus the guarantor of a better covenant."** (Hebrews 7:22 ESV)

The word "guarantor" means "a surety or a pledge". Jesus the heavenly high priest had entered within the veil as their "forerunner," and had now become the guarantee and pledge (the surety payment) of the consummation of the New Covenant. And, in order to establish this truth with those who would be the first fruits of this salvation (2 Thessalonians 2:13), he sent the Holy Spirit as a down payment (additional guarantee) of the inheritance that he would bring at the consummation of that New Covenant. This inheritance was the eternal inheritance promised to Abraham to be received as their consummative New Covenant blessing, and as the perfection and fulfillment of the Law and prophets.

## READY TO VANISH AWAY

**For if that first covenant had been faultless, there would have been no occasion for a second. For he finds fault with them when he says: "The days will come, says the Lord, when I will establish a New Covenant with the house of Israel and with the house of Judah.... This is the covenant that I will make with the house of Israel after those days, says the Lord: I will put my laws into their minds, and write them on their hearts, and I will be their God, and they shall be my people... For I will be merciful toward their iniquities, and I will remember their sins no more. In speaking of a new**

**covenant, he treats the first as obsolete. And what is becoming obsolete and growing old is ready to vanish away.** (Hebrews 8:7-13 RSV)

Notice the present tenses in verse 13. Most translations miss this, but some translations like the one cited, actually translate this properly. No doubt about it, Hebrews 8 makes it clear that at that present time (AD62-64) the Old Covenant had not yet "vanished away". It was "becoming obsolete" and "growing old," and was ready to vanish away.

Let's also take a brief look at the word "establish" in this text.

The Greek word used for "establish" in verse 8 is not the word that one might expect. The word is "*synteleo*" and means "to bring to an end, to complete, to conclude or consummate". I believe this word in the context of the New Covenant carries a two-fold message.

Number one, at this time in redemptive history the New Covenant had already been initiated with the house of Israel and with the house of Judah through the cross. Therefore, for the writer to quote this text from Jeremiah 31 was to say that God had yet to "conclude/consummate" the New Covenant, not initiate it. Number two, when the New Covenant was fully established, it would contain the consummative and completed redemptive blessing for Israel, there would be nothing lacking for man under the New Covenant. In the New Covenant, God's redemption is "finished".

As we have already demonstrated and as Jesus taught, it was through the fulfillment of all prophecy (the Law and prophets) that the changing of the covenants would be fully accomplished. Through His cross and ascension, Jesus had initiated the process of covenantal transition. The New Covenant was in the process of being established and the Old Covenant was in the process of vanishing away, but neither process could be completed until every promise/prophecy (every jot and tittle) contained in the Old Testament was fully accomplished. This would happen in AD 70 through the destruction of Jerusalem in that generation (Luke 21:20-22). To paraphrase the words of the master:

"Fulfillment of all the Law could only come through fulfillment of all prophecy"

"Not an iota, not a dot, will pass from the law until all is accomplished" (Mathew 5:18)

## UNTIL THE TIME OF REFORMATION

Now even the first covenant had regulations for worship and an earthly sanctuary. For a tent was prepared, the outer one, in which were the lampstand and the table and the bread of the Presence; it is called the Holy Place. Behind the second curtain stood a tent called the Holy of Holies.... These preparations having thus been made, the priests go continually into the outer tent, performing their ritual duties, but into the second only the high priest goes, and he but once a year, and not without taking blood which he offers for himself and for the errors of the people. By this the Holy Spirit indicates that the way into the sanctuary is not yet opened as long as the outer tent is still standing, which is symbolic for the present age. According to this arrangement, gifts and sacrifices are offered which cannot perfect the conscience of the worshiper, but deal only with food and drink and various ablutions, regulations for the body imposed (being imposed-present tense) until the time of reformation (Hebrews 9:1-10 RSV)

Before we dig into this text, let's read verses 8-10 in another translation which for the most part translates the verbs in their present tense....

The Holy Spirit is signifying this, that the way into the holy place has not yet been disclosed while the outer tabernacle is still standing, which *is* a symbol for the present time. Accordingly, both gifts and sacrifices are offered which cannot make the worshiper perfect in conscience; since they *relate* only to food and

**drink and various washings, regulations for the body imposed (being imposed - present tense – D.D.) until a time of reformation** (NASB)

Ok, now let's break it down a bit....

The word for "standing" in verse 8 is "stasis" in the Greek and in this context means "covenantal standing/significance".

For example, it appears as such in other translations:

> **.... not yet been disclosed as long as the first tabernacle was still functioning"** (NIV)

The word for "reformation" in verse 10 is *diorthosis* in the Greek and means "restoring to its natural or normal condition, making straight"

Here is how it appears in other translations:

> **".... until the time of restoration..."** (HCSB)
> **"... until a better system to be established"** (NLT)
> **"... until the time of new order..."** (NIV)

Notice just a few of the things that Hebrews 9 teaches:

1. **Throughout Israel's history, while the Old Covenant system (either through tabernacle or temple) was functioning, the system itself**

demonstrated that the people did not have access to the presence of God.

2. That entire Old Covenant system was but a parable (an illustration used to explain something by comparison) for the then-present (first century) time.

3. By being an illustration for the first century, this meant that as long as that Old Covenant system was still in operation and being imposed as a covenantal institution, access into the most holy place (the True and Heavenly Temple of God) was not yet made available to the people of God.

Based on the ground we have covered up to this point this should not surprise us. After all, access into the most holy place is a New Covenant blessing, and as we have seen, the New Covenant was still not fully established/consummated at the time Hebrews was written.

> According to Hebrews 9:10, access would only be granted into the most holy place at the time of reformation, the time of the "new order", that is, the consummation of the New Covenant.

In addition to this, Hebrews 11 teaches that not even the Old Testament faithful had received their inheritance (had obtained access to the most holy place) at the time when Hebrews was written. Furthermore, that access would only be obtained by the faithful community of all ages together, that is, at the same time. (For further study regarding what we have said regarding Hebrews 9, please take the time to compare Leviticus 16:17 with Hebrews 9:11-12,15,24-28 and 11:39-40, all the while keeping in mind that the context of Hebrews 9-11 is the fulfillment of the Day of Atonement – Leviticus 16).

## TAKING AWAY THE FIRST TO ESTABLISH THE SECOND

**For the law having a shadow of the coming good things, not the very image of the matters, every year, by the same sacrifices that they offer continually, is never able to make perfect those coming near** (Hebrews 10:1 YLT)

The first thing we need to see here is once again the present tense of the verse.

**"...the law having a shadow...".**

The writer clearly states that the Law was at that time still a shadow. This is made even more clear by the next part of the verse....

**"...of the coming good things..."**

If the Law was but an earthly shadow of spiritual realities in Christ (which it was-Colossians 2:16-17), then the "coming good things" in this text refer to the consummative redemptive blessings of the New Covenant, which they were already "tasting of" (Hebrews 6:5). Hebrews 10:1 serves as a partial commentary on Hebrews 9:8 as to why the New Covenant was still being "imposed".

> The Old Covenant retained its covenantal standing as a "covenantal institution" as long as it remained the shadow form of what was still yet to come in the New Covenant.

It also continued to serve as a tutor to Israel (and her proselytes), in order to bring them to the faith. (Galatians 3:24-25)

> Then he said, "Behold, I have come to do thy will." He takes away the first, in order to establish the second. (Hebrews 10:9 NASB)

Once again, the interpreters conveniently change the present tense of the Greek verb *"anaireo"*, translated as "take away". This literally reads... "He is taking away the first in order to establish the second". But that's not all, notice the phrase "in order that".

Hebrews 10 teaches that in order for the New Covenant to be "established", the Old Covenant had to first be "taken away". But remember Jesus' golden rule. It would not be taken away until it was all fulfilled (Mathew 5:17-18). Its removal would only come through its fulfillment, and not prior to it.

Hebrews 10 is irrefutable proof that between AD30 and AD 70 the Old Covenant had not yet been removed or fulfilled, nor had the New Covenant yet been fully established (consummated). Therefore, at the time of the writing of Hebrews (approximately 63-64AD), we have demonstrated that:

1. The Law and the prophets (the Old Covenant) were not yet fulfilled at the cross.
   (Mathew 5:17- 18, Acts 24:14-15, Luke 21:22)

2. The Old Covenant had not yet vanished away/become obsolete. (Hebrews 8:13, 10:1,9)

3. Because the Old Covenant had not yet been fulfilled, entrance into the most holy place was not yet available.
   (Hebrews 9, 11:39-40, Leviticus 16:17)

4. Jesus' high priesthood was the guarantee that the New Covenant would soon be established and access into the most holy place made available. (Hebrews 5-7)

5. The New Covenant was not yet fully established. It would only be established when the Old Covenant was fulfilled and taken away. (Hebrews 9-10, Mathew 5:17-18)

> **We have established beyond refutation that the covenants were in "transition" after the cross and prior to AD 70. Thus, a first century "covenantal transition" has been established.**

# CHAPTER TWO

## THE INHERITANCE THROUGH COVENANTAL TRANSITION

**Grace to you and peace from God our Father and the Lord Jesus Christ, who gave Himself for our sins so that He might rescue us from this present evil age, according to the will of our God and Father.** (Galatians 1:3-4 NASB)

Many commentators interpret "this present evil age" as the "wicked and fallen world system" of which we as humans are currently trapped in due to the fall of man. However, I believe this interpretation violates the principle of audience relevance and entirely misses the message of the book of Galatians. As we will demonstrate, what Paul meant by "rescue from the present evil age" was to be completely delivered from the bondage of sin and death under the age of Torah by receiving the inheritance promised to Abraham at the full establishment of the New Covenant age. After all, doesn't the fact of a first century covenantal transition virtually demand that the ages which were represented by those covenants were likewise in transition?

> **In light of the first century covenantal transition, we should understand that their rescue from the then-present evil age would be accomplished at the "end" (the terminative goal) of that evil age in AD 70, through the establishment of the New Covenant age.**

In my opinion, this is the core message of the book of Galatians.

# THE PROMISE OF THE INHERITANCE

> **Christ redeemed us from the curse of the Law, having become a curse for us, for it is written, "cursed is everyone who hangs on a tree", in order that in Christ Jesus the blessing of Abraham might come to the Gentiles, so that we would receive the promise of the Spirit through faith….** (Galatians 3:13-14 NASB)

First, let's understand right away that this text is not teaching that Jesus died so that they could receive the Holy Spirit. (There is an element of truth in that statement, but that's not what this text is teaching, not at all). Jesus' death was so that through faith, they would receive the blessing of Abraham, which was the promise of (made by/through) the Spirit.

In verse 16 Paul refers to the promise as "promises" (plural), denoting that there were multiple promises (renewals of the same promise) made to Abraham and his natural descendants which constituted the one overarching promise. This is confirmed by the return to the singular "promise" in verse 17.

> **Now the promises were spoken to Abraham and to his seed. He does not say, "And to seeds," as**

*referring* to many, but *rather* to one, "And to your seed," that is, Christ. What I am saying is this: the Law, which came four hundred and thirty years later, does not invalidate a covenant previously ratified by God, so as to nullify the promise. (Galatians 3:16-17)

Paul says in verse 17 that the promise was to come through a "covenant", that is, the Abrahamic covenant. In other words, the promise would be received through the fulfillment of the Abrahamic covenant which had been previously ratified by God.

For if the inheritance is based on law, it is no longer based on a promise; but God has granted it to Abraham by means of a promise
(Galatians 3:18 NASB)

Paul could not have been clearer. The promise made to Abraham was the promise of "the inheritance".

So, follow me on this....

Christ redeemed them from the curse of the Law, so that they would receive the promise of the Spirit. (Galatians 3:13-14)

But, the promise of the Spirit was the promise of "the inheritance" (Galatians 3:18)

Therefore, Christ redeemed them from the curse of the Law so that they (Israel) would receive "the inheritance".

Ask yourself this question.
Had Old Covenant Israel or the Church already received the inheritance when Paul wrote Galatians? According to scripture, the answer is no. At that time in redemptive history, what they had received was "the promise" and a "guarantee" of that inheritance.

> **To say that they were still awaiting their inheritance is the same as saying that they did not have access to the most holy place, which as we have seen, they did not (Hebrews 9:1-10).**

> **In him you also, when you heard the word of truth, the gospel of your salvation, and believed in him, were sealed with the promised Holy Spirit, who is the guarantee of our inheritance until we acquire possession of it, to the praise of his glory.** (Ephesians 1:13-14 ESV)

Paul wrote to the Ephesians that the Holy Spirit who had sealed (literally, had marked) them, was the guarantee of their promised inheritance.

**Instead, you will follow the example of those who are going to inherit God's promises because of their faith and endurance.** (Hebrews 6:12 NLT)

In Hebrews 6:12 the word for inherit is in the present tense in the Greek which means that they were at that time in the process of receiving the inheritance. The Young's Literal Translation interprets this accurately.

**That ye may not become slothful, but followers of those who through faith and patient endurance are inheriting the promises.** (Hebrews 6:12 YLT)

**Therefore, he is the mediator of a New Covenant, so that those who are called may receive the promised eternal inheritance, since a death has occurred that redeems them from the transgressions committed under the first covenant** (Hebrews 9:15 ESV)

**And all these, having gained approval through their faith, did not receive what was promised, because God had provided something better for us, so that apart from us they would not be made perfect.** (Hebrews 11:39-40 NASB)

It is undeniable that decades after the cross, those in Christ who had by faith become the seed of Abraham, they like Abraham,

34

had still not received the promised inheritance, but remained heirs of that promise.

> **"And if you belong to Christ, then you are Abraham's descendants, and heirs according to promise"**. (Galatians 3:29 NASB)

God in his infinite wisdom had determined that "all Israel" would inherit the promise together, that is, at the same time. And since the time of the inheritance had not yet come, they waited and groaned for it together. But all this was about to change through the establishment of their New Covenant and the casting out of the old.

## THE ABRAHAMIC INHERITANCE THROUGH THE NEW COVENANT

As we have seen, the inheritance was the promise made to Abraham, and that by faith, those in Christ (Jew and Gentile) had now become true-Israel and heirs to that promised inheritance.

We will now seek to demonstrate when exactly true-Israel received her inheritance of which "fleshly Israel" had refused and judged themselves unworthy. To do this, we turn to Galatians chapter 4.

**Tell me, you who want to be under law, do you not listen to the law? For it is written that Abraham had two sons, one by the bondwoman and one by the free woman. But the son by the bondwoman was born according to the flesh, and the son by the free woman through the promise.** (Galatians 4:21-23 NASB)

Paul begins by contrasting the two sons (seeds) of Abraham through a well known story in Israel's history. Ishmael was born by the slave girl Hagar, which was the result of human effort and intervention, "according to the flesh". In contrast, Isaac was born by the free woman Sarah, as the beginning of God's fulfillment to his promise made to Abraham.

**This is allegorically speaking, for these women are two covenants: one proceeding from Mount Sinai bearing children who are to be slaves; she is Hagar. Now this Hagar is Mount Sinai in Arabia and corresponds to the present Jerusalem, for she is in slavery with her children.** (Galatians 4:24-25)

Now Paul under the inspiration of the Spirit uses Israel's history as an allegory to further explain to his readers who would receive the inheritance by contrasting two covenants, two women, and two sons. Paul says that "these women are two covenants". Hagar represents the Old Covenant which had produced children (nepios - infants) that were slaves under that covenant. According to Paul, the ethnic seed of Abraham (Israel according to the flesh) was in slavery with their mother - the Old Covenant - represented by geographical/earthly Jerusalem.

**But the Jerusalem above is free; she is our mother** (Galatians 4:26)

This "Jerusalem above" is of course the same as the New Jerusalem of Revelation 21:1 and the "Heavenly Jerusalem" of Hebrews 12:22. But remember, the two women represent the two covenants. So, for Paul to say that the "Jerusalem above" was their (those in Christ) mother, was to say that the New Jerusalem (Sarah) was the New Covenant; which as a mother was birthing them into a new world.

**For it is written: Rejoice barren woman who does not bear, break forth and shout, you who are not in labor, for more numerous are the children of the desolate than of the one who has a husband** (Galatians 4:27)

Isaiah 54:1 in its original context was a prophecy of the restoration of Israel after the Babylonian captivity by their typological return to the land, and their future re-marriage to Yahweh under the New Covenant. However, Paul interprets Isaiah 54:1f to refer to Israel's final restoration to their Abrahamic inheritance through their re-marriage to Yahweh as the Church, through the then-present New Covenant.

The "barren woman" here refers to Sarah, the New Covenant. For at that time the New Covenant (Sarah) had not yet bore any children, she was still a barren/childless covenant and therefore "Jerusalem above" was yet uninhabited. Conversely, the one who had a husband was Hagar - the inhabited Old Covenant - who for centuries had borne children according to the flesh.

Paul's analogy of the New Covenant as a barren woman fits perfectly with what he teaches elsewhere. For example, in Romans 8:23-29 we see that not until "the adoption as sons" (the time of inheritance) would those in Christ be "conformed to the image of the Son" and become the "many brethren" of Jesus. Meaning that at that time Jesus still had no brethren in his image since the adoption as sons had not yet taken place. Paul taught the same thing in 2 Corinthians 3:18 when he said the transformation of the body of Christ into the "image of the Son" would not be a completed process until the New Covenant and its glory was fully received.

> **Sarah (the New Covenant) was at that time still "a desolate woman" because the New Covenant itself had not yet been fully consummated and the sons of that covenant had not yet received their full adoption/inheritance - the image of the firstborn.**

But all that was about to change.

> **And you brethren, like Isaac, are children of promise** (Galatians 4:28)

As Isaac was born to become heir of the promise made to Abraham, so were those in Christ to whom Paul was writing. However, unlike Isaac who died not having received the promise (Hebrews 11:39), it was now being received by that first century generation upon whom "ends of the ages had come" (1 Corinthians 10:11). The blessing of Abraham would be the consummative goal (ends-telos) of all ages.

> **But as at that time he who was born according to the flesh persecuted him who was born according to the Spirit, so it is now also** (Galatians 4:30).

As Ishmael the son of the slave woman "mocked" Isaac the son of Sarah, at that present time the children under the Old Covenant (Israel according to the flesh) were persecuting the sons of the New Covenant, those born by the Spirit.

> **But what does the Scripture say? "Cast out" (ekballo – D.D.) the bondwoman and her son, for the son of the bondwoman shall not be an heir with the son of the free woman. So then, brethren, we are not children of a bondwoman, but of the free woman.** (Galatians 4:30-31)

Paul once again quotes from Genesis 21 and applies it to the then present situation regarding the persecution of the body of Christ by Old Covenant Israel, the Ishmael-seed. And why were Hagar and Ishmael "cast out" in Genesis 21? Because the inheritance was to only be received by the son of the free woman. Said another way, the inheritance was reserved for the sons of Sarah – the sons of the New Covenant. This is emphatic and unambiguous language.

The Old Covenant (the bondwoman-Hagar) and Israel after the flesh (the sons of the bondwoman) would be "cast out" so that they would not and could not share in the inheritance of Abraham's seed (those in Christ) according to the promise (Galatians 3:29).

At this point we need to understand several points which teach a covenantal transition in the book of Galatians.

1. There was still at that time two covenants in existence. The Old Covenant had not yet been "cast out" and the New Covenant had not yet been consummated, she was still "barren" (Galatians 4:24-25, 30-31). This agrees perfectly with what we have already seen in Hebrews 8-10 concerning covenantal transition.

2. There could not and would not be two covenants and two seeds (sons) in existence when the inheritance was to be received. Only one son (the son of the freewoman) could inherit the promise. (Galatians 4:30)

3.  The inheritance would be received by the sons of the freewoman (those in Christ) when the New Covenant was established. But, the New Covenant would only be established when the Old Covenant (bondwoman) and her sons (Israel after the flesh) were cast out.

> **Therefore, whenever Israel (after the flesh) was "cast out", was when those in Christ received their Abrahamic inheritance through the New Covenant thereby consummating the process of covenantal transition.**

So, when was Old Covenant Israel cast out?

> **"Listen to another parable. There was a landowner who planted a vineyard and put a wall around it and dug a wine press in it and built a tower, and rented it out to vine-growers and went on a journey. "When the harvest time approached, he sent his slaves to the vine-growers to receive his produce. The vine-growers took his slaves and beat one, and killed another, and stoned a third. "Again, he sent another group of slaves larger than the first; and they did the same thing to them. But afterward he sent his son to them, saying, 'They**

will respect my son.' But when the vine-growers saw the son, they said among themselves, 'This is the heir; come, let us kill him and seize his inheritance.' They took him, and threw him out of the vineyard and killed him. Therefore, when the owner of the vineyard comes, what will he do to those vine-growers?" They said to Him, "He will bring those wretches to a wretched end, and will rent out the vineyard to other vine-growers who will pay him the proceeds at the proper seasons." Jesus said to them, "Did you never read in the Scriptures, "The stone which the builders rejected, this became the chief corner stone, this came about from the Lord and it is marvelous in our eyes". Therefore, I say to you the kingdom of God will be taken away from you and given to a people, producing the fruit of it. And he who falls on this stone will be broken to pieces; but on whomever it falls, it will scatter him like dust." When the chief priests and the Pharisees heard His parables, they understood that He was speaking about them. (Mathew 21:33-45)

This parable of the landowner and the vineyard is no doubt prophetic of the destiny of first century Jerusalem and Judaism at the hands of the Romans in AD 70. Furthermore, it's a reiteration and interpretation of the parable of "Israel the Lord's vineyard" in Isaiah. In Isaiah 5 Israel is pictured as the planting of the Lord's beautiful vineyard who was intended to bring forth much fruit, but only brought forth "worthless grapes". Their destruction and judgment would come at the hands of a ruthless foreign nation. Jesus interprets this prophecy as reaching its fulfillment in the destruction of the men who would kill him, the "Son" of the landowner. When we combine this parable with a teaching Jesus gave in Luke 13, the time for the casting out of Israel is firmly established beyond any doubt.

> **Strive to enter through the narrow door; for many, I tell you, will seek to enter and will not be able. Once the head of the house gets up and shuts the door, and you begin to stand outside and knock on the door, saying, 'Lord, open up to us!' then He will answer and say to you, 'I do not know where you are from.' Then you will begin to say, 'We ate and drank in Your presence, and You taught in our streets'; and He will say, 'I tell you, I do not know where you are from; depart from me all you evildoers.' In that place there will be weeping and gnashing of teeth when you see Abraham and Isaac and Jacob and all the prophets in the kingdom of God, but yourselves being thrown out (ekballo-cast out – D.D.).**
> (Luke 13:24-28)

Notice also that those who would be "cast out" were those who had eaten and drank in His presence, and to whom Jesus had "taught in their streets". It was the first century generation, "they themselves" who would be cast out.

43

> The scripture is clear, the "taking away" of the kingdom from first century Israel would mean that they had been "cast out" of that kingdom. This was the "casting out" of the "sons of the Old Covenant" (Galatians 4:30) which could not share in the kingdom-inheritance of the sons of the New Covenant.

Galatians 4 is Paul's inspired commentary on Jesus' teaching to the Jews in the days of his flesh.

> They answered Him, "We are Abraham's descendants and have never yet been enslaved to anyone; how is it that You say, 'You will become free'? …. (Jesus answered—D.D.), "The slave does not remain in the house forever; the son does remain forever". (John 8:33-35)

The "slaves" (those under the Law-Galatians 4:1-7) would not remain in the "house" forever, but the "sons" (those in Christ-Galatians 4:1-7) would never be "cast out" of the house.

> All that the Father gives Me will come to Me, and the one who comes to Me I will certainly not cast out. (John 6:37)

Old Covenant Jerusalem and her sons according to the flesh were cast out of the kingdom in the judgment and destruction of Judah in AD 70. This was the time when the Jerusalem above (New Jerusalem) was established through the consummation of the New Covenant, and the sons of that New Covenant, being the spiritual-sons of Abraham received the promise and blessing of Abraham as their eternal inheritance in Jesus Christ.

Therefore, we have established that the inheritance of Israel was received through covenantal transition. The implications of this which we will explore later are both staggering and thrilling.

# CHAPTER THREE

## THE KINGDOM THROUGH COVENANTAL TRANSITION

As we have seen in the initial chapter of this work, the book of Hebrews teaches the doctrine of a first century covenantal transition in a most powerful and definitive way. We have also seen in the previous chapter that the book of Galatians teaches conclusively that through the first century covenantal transition, Israel was receiving her Abrahamic inheritance.

In the chapter now before us, we return to the book of Hebrews to demonstrate that the long anticipated Davidic-Messianic kingdom was being received by the righteous remnant of Israel in the first century through covenantal transition, that is, at the consummation of the New Covenant and the full removal of the old.

## FROM ZION TO THE KINGDOM

The book of Hebrews was written to encourage Israel to faithfully finish their second and final exodus which had begun through the cross of Christ, and was now reaching its end nearly forty years later. This exodus was their coming out of the Old Covenant world of Judaism dominated by sin and death, and entering fully into the New Covenant, the kingdom of God wherein dwells righteousness. In chapters 3-4 of Hebrews, Israel's typological inheritance is being contrasted with her true inheritance in Christ. The "rest" which Joshua had given their fathers in Canaan was only typological of the rest that was still available to them, if they would "hold fast the beginning of their assurance firm until the end." The faithful remnant of all   ages was on the verge of receiving their Messianic kingdom-restoration through the New Covenant in Christ.

**Therefore, since we have so great a cloud of witnesses surrounding us, let us also lay aside every encumbrance and the sin which so easily entangles us, and let us run with endurance the race that is set before us.** (Hebrews 12:1)

> **The "race (contest) set before them" was the redemptive-marathon in which all the Old Testament faithful had participated, and were now eagerly awaiting its consummation (Hebrews 11).**

It was now up to that first-fruit-first-century generation empowered by the Spirit to finish the second exodus. Therefore, they were to fix their eyes on Jesus (their forerunner), cast off the sin of apostasy which had entangled so many already, and endure to the "end" of the Old Covenant age. The exodus theme of chapters 3-4 is picked up again in Hebrews 12 as Israel has now come to the end and consummation of her final wilderness testing. This time around, it's not a journey from Sinai to Canaan, but from Zion to the Kingdom. A journey which began at a better mountain and headed towards a better inheritance.

For you have not come to what may be touched, a blazing fire, and darkness, and gloom, and a tempest and the sound of a trumpet, and a voice whose words made the hearers entreat that no further messages be spoken to them. For they could not endure the order that was given, "If even a beast touches the mountain, it shall be stoned. Indeed, so terrifying was the sight that Moses said, "I tremble with fear". (Hebrews 12:18-21)

This portion of the text is a direct illusion to Exodus 19 when Israel received the Old Covenant at Sinai following her deliverance from Egypt.

You shall set bounds for the people all around, saying, "Beware that you do not go up on the mountain or touch the border of it, whoever touches the mountain shall surely be put to death...he shall surely be stoned or shot through, whether beast or man, he shall not live...Now Mount Sinai was all in smoke because the Lord descended upon it in fire, and its smoke ascended like the smoke of a furnace, and the whole mountain quaked violently. When the sound of the trumpet grew louder and louder, Moses spoke and God answered him with thunder. (Exodus.19:12-19)

What is significant about Mount Sinai is that it was the place where God made the Old Covenant with Israel after he had delivered them from Egypt. This is seen earlier in Exodus 19.

> "... Thus, you shall say to the house of Jacob and tell the sons of Israel: "You yourselves have seen what I did to the Egyptians, and how I bore you on eagle's wings, and brought you to myself. Now then, if you will indeed obey my voice and keep my covenant, then you shall be my own possession among all the peoples for all the earth is mine. And you shall be to me a kingdom of priests and a holy nation.... All the people answered together and said, "All that the Lord has spoken we will do..." (Exodus 19:3-8)

Now, although the Old Covenant was initiated at Sinai near the beginning of the wilderness wanderings, it wasn't until nearly forty years (one generation) later when Israel stood in Moab ready to enter the promised land and receive their inheritance, that they "entered into" that covenant and were "established" as the Lord's people.

> These are the words of the covenant which the Lord commanded Moses to make with the sons of Israel in the Land of Moab, besides the covenant which he had made with them in Horeb.... You stand today, all of you, before the Lord your God.... That you may enter into   the

covenant with the Lord your God, and into his oath which the Lord your God is making with you today, in order that he may establish you today as his people and that he may be your God, just as he spoke to you and as he swore to your fathers, to Abraham, Isaac, and Jacob. (Deuteronomy 29:1, 10-12)

> Israel received her inheritance through an initiation-to-consummation (already-but-not-yet) process in the Old Covenant - from Sinai to Canaan.

This is significant because this is precisely what the writer of Hebrews is contrasting in chapter 12. The contrast is not that one covenant began at Mount Sinai and the other was consummating in Mount Zion, that would hardly be a contrast. Instead, the contrast is the two places of covenant-initiation, Sinai and Zion. The typological connection that the writer of Hebrews is making is powerful.

The Old Covenant was received from Sinai.... the New Covenant from Zion. The Old Covenant was "established and entered into" at the end of the forty years.... the New Covenant was being fully established and "entered into" at the end of the forty years.

Canaan was inherited through the establishment of the Old Covenant.... the Kingdom was being inherited through the establishment of the New Covenant, that is, through covenantal transition.

One last point before we move on. The phrase ".... what may be touched" in Hebrews 12:18 indicates something tangible and physical. Said another way, the Old Covenant had an "earthly sanctuary" (Hebrews 9:1) and could therefore be "shaken" and "removed". However, the mountain and the covenant to which this first century generation had come was of an altogether different nature.

> **..... But you have come to Mount Zion, and to the city of the living God, the heavenly Jerusalem, and to innumerable angels in festal gathering and to the assembly of the first-born who are enrolled in heaven, and to God the judge of all, and to the spirits of just men made perfect and to Jesus, the mediator of a New Covenant, and to the sprinkled blood that speaks more graciously than the blood of Abel.** (Hebrews 12:2-24)

So how and when was the New Covenant initiated from Mount Zion? And when did Israel come (arrive) to Mount Zion? Scripture is clear that at the ascension, Jesus was seated on David's throne at the right hand of the Father in fulfillment of Psalm 110. However, according to Psalm 110, to be seated on David's throne meant that Jesus was "ruling from Zion".

> **"And so, because he was a prophet and knew that God had sworn to him with an oath, to seat one of his descendants on his throne…. Therefore, having been exalted to the right hand of God, and having received from the Father the promise of the Holy Spirit, He has poured forth this which you both see and hear. "For it was not David who ascended into heaven, but he himself says: The Lord said to my Lord, sit at my right hand until I make your enemies a footstool for your feet.** (Acts 2:30-34)

> **The Lord says to my Lord: "Sit at My right hand until I make Your enemies a footstool for Your feet." The Lord will stretch forth your strong scepter from Zion, saying "rule in the midst of your enemies"** (Psalm 110:1-2)

We see the same thing in the book of Hebrews. At his ascension, Jesus became the "begotten Son of God" in fulfillment of Psalm 2. Jesus had entered into his King-Priestly ministry and was declared the Son of God as the "firstborn Son" from the dead. However, according to Psalm 2, by Jesus entering into his preeminent Son-ship, this meant that Jesus had been installed as Yahweh's King upon Mount Zion.

**So also Christ did not glorify Himself so as to become a high priest, but He who said to Him, "You are my Son, today I have begotten you"**
(Hebrews 5:5)

**But as for Me, I have installed My King upon Zion, My holy mountain." "I will surely tell of the decree of the Lord: He said to Me, 'You are My Son, today I have begotten You.**
(Psalm 2:6-7)

So, consider the following:

Israel received the Old Covenant at Sinai 50 days after their deliverance from Egypt by the blood of the Passover lamb, through the mediation of Moses
(Exodus 20:18-19, Galatians 3:19)

True-Israel (the Church) received the New Covenant 50 days after their deliverance from sin by the blood of the perfect Passover Lamb, through the mediation of Jesus.
(Acts 2:33, Hebrews 9:15)

However, since Jesus was ruling as King of Israel from Mount Zion when the New Covenant was initiated, this means that True-Israel received their New Covenant through the mediation of Jesus, from Mount Zion.

> **They had come to Jesus the mediator of the New Covenant, and in doing so, they had come to Mount Zion. It was to this event that Hebrews 12:22 refers.**

Jeremiah prophesied of the time when Israel would come to Mount Zion to receive the everlasting covenant. The writer of Hebrews tells us that Jeremiah's everlasting covenant was the covenant through which Jesus himself was raised, clearly the New Covenant.

> **They will ask for the way to Zion, turning their faces in its direction; they will come that they may join themselves to the Lord in an everlasting covenant that will not be forgotten.** (Jeremiah 50:5)

> **Now the God of peace, who brought up from the dead the great shepherd of the sheep through the blood of the eternal covenant, even Jesus our Lord.** (Hebrews 13:20)

By coming to Mount Zion and the New Covenant, they were being allowed to experience the glories of that covenant through the Spirit. Therefore, from Pentecost until the time when Hebrews was written, they had been "tasting of the powers of the age to come" (Hebrews 6:5). We should make one last point before we move on. When the writer of Hebrews says "you have come to Mount Zion", he is quoting directly from Isaiah 35. Now, what is so powerful about this is that Isaiah's prophecy is clearly a prophecy of the consummative restoration and salvation of Israel at the coming of the Lord in glory.

> **And the ransomed of the LORD shall return, and come to Zion with songs and everlasting joy upon their heads: they shall obtain joy and gladness, and sorrow and sighing shall flee away.** (Isaiah 35:10)

By coming to Zion, the writer of Hebrews is saying in the most emphatic way that Israel had begun their second and new exodus. Israel had been redeemed (ransomed), had returned to Zion, and would soon receive their inheritance. Isaiah 35 was being fulfilled.

# A COVENANTAL SHAKING

As we continue in Hebrews, what follows next is the writer's last plea to his Hebrew readers to not make the same mistake as their fathers by refusing the gospel of him who was speaking and now warning them from heaven. The blessings of Mount Zion had been experienced through the Spirit for nearly forty years, and the time for "tasting only" was coming to an end. It was now time for Israel to cross over and enter their inheritance to receive the full glory of the New Covenant.

Having contrasted the two "exodus beginnings" as the "two places" of covenantal-initiation, the writer of Hebrews now goes on to contrast "the final warnings" given to Israel at the end of their exodus journeys and the time of covenantal-consummation.

> ...See to it that you do not refuse him who is speaking. For if they did not escape when they refused him who warned them on earth, much less shall we escape if we reject him who warns from heaven (Hebrews 12:25)

The obvious contrast is between Moses and Christ. Moses was the messenger from earth, who warned them on earth, Christ was the messenger from heaven, who warned them from heaven. But this verse is also a reiteration of Hebrews chapter 2:1-3.

> For this reason we must pay much closer attention to what we have heard, so that we do not drift away from it. For if the word spoken through angels proved unalterable, and every transgression and disobedience received a just penalty how will we escape if we neglect so great a salvation? After it was at the first spoken through the Lord, it was confirmed to us by those who heard. (Hebrews 2:1-3)

The first and the last warnings in the book of Hebrews are parallels, and form a powerful inclusio within the book. The message the writer is conveying is clear. Since justice was meted out as the penalty for every disobedience to the words and warnings of the angels spoken by Moses-words which could never bring salvation, then there would be no escape for those who proved disobedient to the words and warnings of Jesus and his apostles-words which if obeyed, would bring salvation. By rejecting Him who was warning from heaven, they not only destined themselves for judgment, but worse, they were neglecting His great salvation.

But that's not it, as we already alluded, Hebrews 12:25 is also an echo back to the words of Moses when Israel had come to the end of their forty- year exodus journey and were about to "enter into" the covenant previously initiated at Sinai.

> **For if you turn away from following Him, He will
> once more abandon them in the wilderness,
> and you will destroy all these people."**
> (Numbers 32:15)

In Numbers 32, Moses warned the new (second) wilderness-generation that if they were to turn back again and refuse to enter their inheritance then God would "once more abandon and destroy them in the wilderness", just as he had done to the original exodus generation. The writer of Hebrews is reminding his readers of Moses' words. Moses gave that generation a "final warning on earth" just before they crossed over to possess their inheritance in Canaan. And now, as the first century generation approached the end of their exodus, and stood as it were on the brink of the Jordan about to inherit the promise, Jesus was giving them a "final warning from heaven". This warning was the message of the book of Hebrews, that the Old Covenant "world" of types and shadows was being shaken and would soon disappear", and those who turned back to it would forfeit the age to come.

**His voice then shook the earth; but now he has promised, "Yet once more I will shake not only the earth but also the heaven** (Hebrews 12:26)

The writer now contrasts the previous "literal" shaking at Sinai (Exodus 19:18) when God gave Israel the Old Covenant, with the then-present "covenantal shaking" of that Old Covenant "world" which was about to be removed. This time, the shaking was not to initiate the Old Covenant, but to remove the old and to consummate the new.

> **In the Old Testament, the "shaking of heaven and earth" was a common metaphor for the Lord's judgment upon Israel or another nation which would bring about a change in government or administration. In some cases, the judgment would result in the deliverance of the nation which was being oppressed by the nation being judged.**

Here are a few examples:

> **Blow a trumpet in Zion, and sound an alarm on My holy mountain! Let all the inhabitants of the land tremble, for the day of the Lord is coming; surely it is near... Before them the earth quakes, the heavens tremble, the sun and the moon grow dark and the stars lose their brightness. The Lord utters His voice before His army; surely His camp is very great, for strong is he who carries out His word. The day of the Lord is indeed great and very awesome, and who can endure it?** (Joel 2:1, 10-11)

In Joel 2 the **"shaking of heaven and earth"** refers to Yahweh's near judgment of Israel in the "day of the Lord" at the hand of a foreign nation (probably Assyria), because they "turned away their heart from the Lord" (v.12). Although judgment would come, the tables would eventually be turned and Israel would be restored and vindicated when the Lord had pity and mercy upon his people (v.18).

In the very next chapter, Joel uses the same language of **"the trembling of the heavens and earth"** to refer to the judgment of the nations (through the judgment of Israel) and the vindication of his elect, whom they had "scattered among the nations". This judgment-shaking brought about a change in Israel's divine order. This shaking would transform Jerusalem from a physical-geographical entity to a spiritual and heavenly entity, where only citizens of the city would be welcome; "strangers" would pass through no more.

> For behold, in those days and at that time, when I restore the fortunes of Judah and Jerusalem, I will gather all the nations and bring them down to the valley of Jehoshaphat. Then I will enter into judgment with them there on behalf of My people and My inheritance, Israel, whom they have scattered among the nations; and they have divided up My land... The sun and moon grow dark and the stars lose their brightness. The Lord roars from Zion and utters His voice from Jerusalem, and the heavens and the earth tremble. But the Lord is a refuge for His people and a stronghold to the sons of Israel. Then you will know that I am the Lord your God, dwelling in Zion, my holy mountain. So Jerusalem will be holy, and strangers will pass through it no more. (Joel 3:1-2, 15-17)

Next are the words of Isaiah.

> The word which Isaiah the son of Amoz saw concerning Judah and Jerusalem.... For You have abandoned Your people, the house of Jacob, because they are filled with influences from the east, and they are soothsayers like the Philistines, and they strike bargains with the children of foreigners.... Men will go into caves

**of the rocks and into holes of the ground before
the terror of the Lord and the splendor of His
majesty, when He arises to make the earth
tremble... In order to go into the caverns of the
rocks and the clefts of the cliffs before the terror
of the Lord and the splendor of His majesty,
when He arises to make the earth tremble.**
(Isaiah 2:1, 6, 19-20)

In the context of Isaiah 2, the "shaking of the earth" referred to
the Lord's "last days" judgment on Judah. These last days were
historically the time of "governmental change" (that is,
Messianic change) for Israel, when "the Law" and the "word of
the Lord" (the gospel) would flow from Zion, the new Jerusalem.

Let's look at another example from Isaiah:

**The oracle concerning Babylon which Isaiah the
son of Amoz saw.... Behold, the day of the Lord
is coming, cruel, with fury and burning anger, to
make the land a desolation; and He will
exterminate its sinners from it. For the stars of
heaven and their constellations will not flash
forth their light; the sun will be dark when it
rises and the moon will not shed its light....
Therefore, I will make the heavens tremble, and
the earth will be shaken from its place at the
fury of the Lord of hosts in the day of His
burning anger.** (Isaiah 13:1, 9-13)

In Isaiah 13 the **"shaking of heaven and earth"** is metaphoric language which referred to the imminent judgment of Babylon at the hands of the Medes. This event historically took place while Daniel the prophet was in Babylonian exile. Clearly this "shaking" was not a literally cosmic event. It is interesting to note that this "judgment-shaking" of Babylon led to the typological return and restoration of Israel under the Median and Persian empire. This "shaking of heaven and earth" represented not only the judgment of the Lord, but a change in administration and government as the Medes replaced Babylon as the new world power.

Even King David used this metaphoric expression as an illustration of what was transpiring through his own personal experience.

> **For the choir director. A psalm of David the servant of the Lord, who spoke to the Lord the words of this song in the day that the Lord delivered him from the hand of all his enemies and from the hand of Saul. And he said, "I love You, O Lord, my strength."…. In my distress I called upon the Lord, and cried to my God for help; He heard my voice out of His temple, and my cry for help before Him came into His ears…**
> **. Then the earth shook and quaked; and the foundations of the mountains were trembling and were shaken, because He was angry. Smoke**

**went up out of His nostrils, and fire from His mouth devoured; coals were kindled by it….He bowed the heavens also, and came down with thick darkness under His feet…. He sent out His arrows, and scattered them, and lightning flashes in abundance, and routed them…. He delivered me from my strong enemy, and from those who hated me, for they were too mighty for me.** (Psalm 18:1,6-9,14,17)

David uses the same language of "cosmic shakings" to refer to Yahweh's judgment of his enemies and his deliverance from them. And, this "shaking" also pointed to a change in Divine administration and order which took place when the "house of David" replaced "house of Saul".

Clearly, none of the above texts refer to a "literal shaking" of the heavens and earth, nor would the original readers of those texts have understood those words in that literal sense. Rather, the "shaking" of the heavens and earth was common metaphorical language which referred to the judgment of a nation, often in connection with a change in governmental power and administration, which Yahweh often used for the purpose of the deliverance and restoration of his covenant people Israel.

In other words...

In the Old Testament scriptures the imagery of "cosmic disturbance / destruction" was a common way to communicate that political or social change was coming through the destruction/judgment of a nation in order to bring restoration and deliverance to the covenant people of God.

This is exactly the message that we find in Haggai chapter 2, one of the Old Testament sources of Hebrews 12:26.

For thus says the Lord of hosts, 'Once more in a little while, I am going to shake the heavens and the earth, the sea also and the dry land. 'I will shake all the nations; and they will come with the wealth of all nations, and I will fill this house with glory,' says the Lord of hosts…. Speak to Zerubbabel governor of Judah, saying, 'I am going to shake the heavens and the earth. 'I will overthrow the thrones of kingdoms and destroy the power of the kingdoms of the nations; and I will overthrow the chariots and their riders, and the horses and their riders will go down, everyone by the sword of another.'
(Haggai 2:6-7, 21-22)

In Haggai chapter 2, the **"shaking of heaven and earth"** referred to the typological restoration of Israel from Babylon captivity, climaxing in the beautification of the temple by Herod the Great. However, the writer of the book of Hebrews interprets this shaking of heaven and earth to refer to the final (once more) shaking and removing of the Old Covenant world system, and the final restoration of Israel through the establishment of the New Covenant order.

Based on the above texts, and specifically the context of Haggai 2 as the source of Hebrews 12:26, it's important that we be consistent and apply this biblical understanding of the "shaking of heaven and earth" to Hebrews 12. This becomes especially important in view of the overall context of the book of Hebrews (the changing of divine administrations, through the judgment of those who refused to accept that change, and the vindication of those who did accept it).

**What this means is when we come to Hebrews 12, we should understand the "shaking of heaven and earth" to mean that the Old Covenant world was in the process of being replaced by the New Covenant world, and that God's judgment would come upon those who resisted that change. But to those who received it, it would be their restoration and their transformation.**

# RECEIVING AN UNSHAKABLE KINGDOM

**…. This phrase, "Yet once more," indicates the removal of what is shaken, as of what has been made, in order that what cannot be shaken may remain.** (Hebrews 12:27)

The first thing we should note is that the Greek word for "shaken" is in the present tense. This means that what was soon to be removed was at that time already being shaken. At this point, there should be no doubt that what was being shaken and removed was the Old Covenant, and by implication the entire "Old Covenant world". This agrees perfectly with what we have seen already in the book of Hebrews.

In Hebrews 8 the Old Covenant was "becoming obsolete and growing old" and was "ready to vanish away" (8:13), which as we saw in Hebrews 10, could only "be taken away" when the second (New) Covenant was "established" (10:9). This is precisely why Hebrews 7 says that Jesus was the "guarantor of the better covenant" (7:22). His high priesthood guaranteed the new administration which had not yet fully arrived.

In other words, the Old Covenant (that which could be touched-which had been made) was being shaken through covenantal transition and would finally be removed at the consummation and establishment of the New Covenant. This was taking place in order that the New Covenant which can never be shaken would "remain".

There is a powerful parallel between Hebrews 12 and 2 Corinthians 3 concerning this word "remain" (meno).

> **For if the ministry of condemnation has glory, much more does the ministry of righteousness abound in glory. For indeed what had glory, in this case has no glory because of the glory that surpasses it. (NKJV) For if what is passing away was glorious, what remains is much more glorious.** (2 Corinthians 3:9-11)

When contrasting the Old and New Covenants in 2 Corinthians 3, Paul says that the Old Covenant was "passing away" and the New Covenant was what would "remain" (*meno*).

When contrasting the Old and New Covenants in Hebrews 12, the writer says that what was "being shaken" would be "removed" and what "could not be shaken" would "remain" (*meno*).

Should there really be any doubt that what was "ready to vanish away" (Hebrews 8:13) and what was "being shaken" and "removed" (Hebrews 12:27), was the Old Covenant that was "passing away" as per 2 Corinthians 3:11?

And, should there really be any doubt that what was being "guaranteed" (Hebrews 7:22), being "established" (Hebrews 10:9), and "could not be shaken" but would "remain" (Hebrews 12:27,) was the New Covenant that would "remain" as per 2 Corinthians 3:11?

I would sincerely hope not, as the connection is far too obvious to ignore. That being the case, the next verse is the divine commentary and interpretation of what those first century believers were receiving in the New Covenant, that is, through covenantal transition.

> **…. Therefore, since we are receiving a kingdom which cannot be shaken, let us have grace, by which we may serve God acceptably with reverence and godly fear.** (Hebrews 12:28)

The New Covenant which could not be shaken and was remaining, was the unshakable Kingdom of God. What was remaining is what was being received… and what did remain, has been received.

As we close this chapter, let's look at an Old Testament text which probably served as the primary source for the writer's idea of "the saints receiving the kingdom" in Hebrews 12:28.

> **But the saints of the most High shall take the kingdom, and possess the kingdom forever, even for ever and ever…. Until the Ancient of days came, and judgment was given to the saints of the Most High; and the time came that the saints possessed the kingdom…. And the kingdom and dominion, and the greatness of the kingdom under the whole heaven, shall be given to the people of the saints of the most**

High, whose kingdom is an everlasting kingdom,
and all dominions shall serve and obey him.
(Dan.7:18,22,27)

By "receiving a kingdom" (Hebrews 12:28), Israel was receiving Daniel's Messianic Kingdom, which the "Son of Man" would establish at his "coming in glory" – in the first century. (Daniel 7:13-14, Mathew 16:27-28)

---

**Daniel 7 was being fulfilled, and the Messianic Kingdom was being consummated through covenantal transition.**

---

We will close this chapter with this last thought. I believe that Hebrews 12:18-29 is an inspired commentary on the following from Amos chapter 9.

> Are you not as the sons of Ethiopia to Me, O sons of Israel?" declares the Lord. "Have I not brought up Israel from the land of Egypt, and the Philistines from Caphtor, and the Arameans from Kir? Behold, the eyes of the Lord God are on the sinful kingdom, and I will destroy it from the face of the earth; nevertheless, I will not totally destroy the house of Jacob," declares the Lord. For behold, I am commanding, and I will shake the house of Israel among all nations as grain is shaken in a sieve, but not a kernel will

**fall to the ground. All the sinners of My people will die by the sword, those who say, 'The calamity will not overtake or confront us. In that day I will raise up the fallen booth of David, and wall up its breaches; I will also raise up its ruins and rebuild it as in the days of old.**
(Amos 9:7-11)

The shaking of the Old Covenant was in reality the shaking of the House of Israel. The kernels that would not fall to the ground were the righteous remnant who withstood the shaking of their Old Covenant by "entering into" the New Covenant to become the "booth of David" which was being raised up in Christ (Acts 15:13-18). These righteous kernels received the kingdom through covenantal transition in AD 70.

But the chaff which was shaken as in a sieve and scattered by the wind of the Spirit, was apostate Israel after the flesh, who by refusing to be joined to the New Covenant, were destroyed when their Old Covenant kingdom-world was fully shaken and removed in AD 70.

> **The transition of the covenants in the first century was not only the changing of two ages, the changing of two "seeds" and the changing of two kingdoms. As we shall see next, it was also the changing of two images.**

Thus, we have demonstrated that the eschatological Messianic Kingdom was in fact received through the first century covenantal transition.

# CHAPTER FOUR

## THE IMAGE OF GOD RESTORED THROUGH COVENANTAL TRANSITION

# SEALED FOR THE NEW COVENANT

In my opinion, 2 Corinthians 3 like Hebrews 8-10, is a definitive New Testament teaching of "covenantal transition" prior to AD 70. But before we jump in, we should briefly study a text in chapter 1 which I believe sets the context for chapter 3.

> **But as God is faithful, our word to you is not yes and no…. For as many as are the promises of God, in Him they are yes; therefore, also through Him is our Amen to the glory of God through us. Now He who establishes us with you in Christ and anointed us is God who also sealed us and gave us the Spirit in our hearts as a pledge.** (2 Corinthians 1:18-22)

Paul says that all of God's promises which they had proclaimed through their word (the gospel), had found fulfillment in Christ. This means two things. First, that Jesus as forerunner had already received all the blessings and promises of the New Covenant which were promised under the Old Covenant. And second, that in Christ (in his New Covenant) is where the fulfillment of all those promises are found for his Church (Israel).

Regarding this second point, Paul says **"also through him is our Amen"**. Paul was saying that "what had already been received by Jesus (all New Covenant promises), will also be received by us. Thus, through Jesus was their "amen of faith", their "let it be to us", in anticipation of the New Covenant promises made to "the fathers" under the Old Covenant. Another important point

74

is that the word "establishes" in verse 12 is in the present tense in the Greek. Therefore, according to the context, Paul was saying that God was at that present time "establishing" the Corinthians in all of God's promises. And as proof that they were in fact being established (being brought to a state of completion/maturity) in those promises, they had been sealed by the Holy Spirit who was given as a "pledge" (a down payment of guarantee).

This sets the context for chapter 3. We will now seek to demonstrate that through covenantal transition (the transition from the Old to the New Covenant), true Israel was being established in God's Old Covenant promises, under the New Covenant. In other words, the "Spirit-pledge" was only given and needed until the promised New Covenant was fully established. Thus, the consummation of the New Covenant would be the full establishment of the body of Christ in the Old Covenant promises of God.

> **"By receiving the promises of the Old Covenant, they were receiving the "glory" of the New.**

# COVENANTAL TRANSITION IN 2 CORINTHIANS 3

**…. Not that we are adequate in ourselves to consider anything as coming from ourselves, but our adequacy is from God, who also made us adequate as servants of a New Covenant, not of the letter but of the Spirit; for the letter kills, but the Spirit gives life.** (2 Corinthians 3:5-6)

In verse 6, Paul begins to contrast the "natures" of the two covenants.

The Old Covenant was in "the letter", that is, it's external in nature. It's for the natural man, the old man, the man that is external (outside) of Christ.

The New Covenant is in "the Spirit", that is, it is of the Spirit and internal in nature. It is for the spiritual man, the new man in the image of Christ.

Then in verses 7-10, Paul contrasts the "glories" of the two covenants.

> **…. But if the ministry of death, in letters engraved on stones, came with glory, so that the sons of Israel could not look intently at the face of Moses because of the glory of his face, fading**

**as it was, how will the ministry of the Spirit fail to be even more with glory? For if the ministry of condemnation has glory, much more does the ministry of righteousness abound in glory. For indeed what had glory, in this case has no glory because of the glory that surpasses it.**
(2 Corinthians 3:7-10)

Paul says that the "ministry of condemnation" (Old Covenant) did in fact have glory, but the "ministry of righteousness" (the New Covenant) "abounded" and "surpassed" that glory. So much did the new surpass the old, it was as if the old had no glory at all. I suppose that it is only fitting that the glory of the old which was "fading", should be not worthy to be compared to that coming glory which would remain forever.

Now what is interesting, is that most commentaries lack the proper tense-translation of the Greek verb *katargeo* in verse 11. *Katargeo* is poorly translated as "that which fades away" in the NASB cited below.

> **…. For if that which fades away was with glory, much more that which remains is in glory.**
> (2 Corinthians 3:11)

However, *katargeo* is in the present tense and should be translated accordingly. This means that the NASB and many other translations have it wrong. Both the NKJV and YLT translate it correctly.

**For if what is passing away was glorious, what remains is much more glorious.** (NKJV)

**For if that which is being made useless is through glory, much more that which is remaining is in glory** (YLT)

By translating this one word properly, it totally changes the meaning of the verse, and the entire chapter. Apostle Paul is teaching (nearly 30 years after the cross) that the Old Covenant was still in the process of "passing away", it was at that time "being made useless".

> **2 Corinthians 3 teaches clearly and irrefutably that the covenants were in a state of transition in the first century.**

This also validates what we said earlier in this chapter, that the New Covenant and its promises were at that time still being "established". The reason that the promises were still being established and had not yet been fully received, was because the covenant itself in which those promises found fulfillment, had not yet been established either. Notice in the same verse that Paul also contrasts the temporal and the eternal standings of the two covenants.

The Old Covenant, the "ministry of death" was "fading away" (v.7, 11). The Old Covenant was therefore transient and temporal, and was from its beginning destined to fade away (v.13). But the New Covenant, the "ministry of righteousness" was "remaining" (v.11). It is the Everlasting Covenant (Hebrews 13:20) which is eternal and heavenly, and which will never be removed. (Hebrews 12:28)

> …. Therefore, having such a hope, we use great boldness in our speech, and are not like Moses, who used to put a veil over his face so that the sons of Israel would not look intently at the end of what was fading away. (2 Corinthians 3:13)

Although we have dealt with this already, it never hurts to emphasize this point. The Old Covenant was never intended to be "instantly" removed/abolished at the cross in a "twinkling of an eye event".

---

The "fading of the glory" on Moses' face pointed to the fact that the Old Covenant and its glory would one day "fade away", that is, it would be removed through a gradual process - a transition.

---

Notice also that Moses veiled his face so that Israel could not see the "end" of which that glory represented. The Greek word for "end" is "telos" which means end or completion, but carries with it the idea of a goal or a purpose. Moses's veil was preventing Israel from seeing the end-goal and purpose of that Old Covenant glory - which was the New Covenant and its greater glory. In other words, that veil kept them "shut up to the faith", which was now about to be revealed.

(Galatians 3:23)

> **.... But to this day whenever Moses is read, a veil lies over their heart; but whenever a person turns to the Lord, the veil is taken away. Now the Lord is the Spirit, and where the Spirit of the Lord is, there is liberty. But we all, with unveiled face, beholding as in a mirror the glory of the Lord, are being transformed into the same image from glory to glory, just as from the Lord, the Spirit.** (2 Corinthians 3:15-18)

We see here a contrast in "heart" between Israel according to the flesh and Israel in Christ.

The hearts of those Old Covenant Jews were veiled through their rejection of Christ, and that veiling of the heart was their bondage. But the hearts of those who had put their faith in Christ had been opened, and their "face" had been unveiled to reflect His glorious freedom. Their hearts had been circumcised.

The phrase "beholding as in a mirror" means to look/see as through the reflection of glass, or a mirror. Paul is again making another powerful contrast here.

Moses' veiled face prevented Israel from seeing the glory of the New Covenant (the end-goal of the Old Covenant). But, the unveiled face of those in Christ who were reflecting the glory of Christ and His New Covenant, were allowing Israel to see the "end" (the purposed goal) of her Old Covenant form. Only in Christ could Israel see that the New Covenant was the prophetic consummation and destiny of the Old.

## THE IMAGE OF THE NEW COVENANT

As we come to the climax of chapter 3, let's look at verse 18 again for emphasis sake.

> **But we all, with unveiled face, beholding as in a mirror the glory of the Lord, are being transformed into the same image from glory to glory, just as from the Lord, the Spirit.**
> (2 Corinthians 3:18)

Now, I was taught for years that this phrase "from glory to glory" was a generic term that could be applied to just about anything. For example, if my marriage was not so good last year, but slightly improved the next, then I was going from "glory to glory".

If I struggled with a certain issue in one area of my life, but by God's grace was able to overcome it, then I had gone from "glory to glory". I'm guessing that this interpretation/application of this text is familiar with most people. However, the context of 2 Corinthians 3 will not allow for any such arbitrary application.

What we will learn next is very powerful and very profound, and has massive implications regarding the "glory texts" of the New Testament - a rabbit trail which cannot be followed in this work. However, what follows is in my opinion paradigmatic for many such texts.

Based on the context of the entire chapter, the phrase "from glory to glory" refers to the glory of the two covenants that Paul had contrasted in verses 7-10. There is absolutely no way that we can contextually make this "glory" refer anything but the glory of the Old and New Covenants.

As the remnant of Israel was leaving behind the lesser glory of the Old Covenant and entering the greater glory of the New, they were being transformed into the "image" of the Lord through the eschatological work of the Spirit. Said another way, Israel (and through Israel, mankind) was being restored into the image of God through covenantal transition.

> **By transitioning from one covenant to another, Israel was likewise transitioning from one corporate man to another, from one corporate glory to another, and therefore, from one corporate image to another.**

By putting off the "old man" (Ephesians 4:22), they were putting off the image of the first man, Adam (1 Corinthians 15:49), who is the image of the Old Covenant (2 Corinthians 3:18). And by putting on the "new man" (Ephesians 4:24), they were being clothed in the image of the last Adam, Christ (Romans 8:29, 1 Corinthians 15:49, 2 Corinthians 3:18, 5:1-5), who is the image of the New Covenant. (2 Corinthians 3:18).

The power of 2 Corinthians 3 is that it teaches that **covenantal transition was the process and method by which man was being restored into the image of God in Christ, which had been lost in Eden.** Covenantal transition was God's Spirit-empowered eschatological vehicle that transformed man from the image of a beast lost in sin, into the image of the Son without sin. Therefore, since the Old Covenant has passed and the New Covenant has arrived, then undeniably, covenantal transition has been accomplished and man's transformation into the image of Christ completed.

Thus, man was restored to the image of God through covenantal transition. The implications of this fact are truly life changing. In the final chapter to follow, we will explore the implications of the truths expressed in each of the previous chapters.

# CHAPTER FIVE

## THE IMPLICATIONS OF A FIRST CENTURY COVENANTAL TRANSITION

In chapter 1 **we established beyond any shadow of doubt that the Old and New Covenants were in transition during the first century, specifically between AD30 and AD 70.** What follows logically from that truth is this:

> **Since the covenants were in transition, the consummative and redemptive elements of those covenants were likewise in transition at the same time.**

Throughout this work we have looked at three of those redemptive elements; the inheritance, the kingdom, and the image of God. These elements were received by Israel through covenantal transition when the Old Covenant, after serving its prophetic purpose, was fully accomplished and passed away. At that time, the New Covenant was fully established and consummated. This transition was consummated in AD 70.

We demonstrated this to be true in chapters 2 through 4.

In chapter 2 we established that **the inheritance of Israel was received through covenantal transition.**

In chapter 3 we established that **the Kingdom of Israel was restored through covenantal transition.**

And, in chapter 4 we established that **the image of God was received and restored through covenantal transition.**

In this final chapter, we will explore the significance and the implications of each of these truths.

## THE IMPLICATIONS OF THE INHERITANCE THROUGH COVENANTAL TRANSITION

Why is it significant that what scripture calls "the inheritance" was received in the first century through covenantal transition, and what is the implication for us today? As we shall demonstrate below, since the inheritance was received through covenantal transition in the first century, this means that the "second coming" (Parousia) of the Lord was also a first century event which (as we shall see) consummated salvation. We must understand that the receiving of the inheritance cannot be separated from the coming of the Savior.

The prophet Isaiah spoke of "a covenant" which would bring the inheritance, in the "day of salvation" (also see Isaiah 60).

> **Thus says the Lord, "In a favorable time I have answered You, And in a day of salvation I have helped You; And I will keep You and give You for a covenant of the people, To restore the land, to make them inherit the desolate heritages.** (Isaiah 49:8)

Said another way, the inheritance would come at the time of salvation. This is an important fact that is expounded upon in the New Testament and reiterated by the apostles, who spoke nothing but what Moses and the prophets said would take place.

> **Blessed be the God and Father of our Lord Jesus Christ, who according to His great mercy has caused us to be born again to a living hope through the resurrection of Jesus Christ from the dead, to obtain an inheritance which is imperishable and undefiled and will not fade away, reserved in heaven for you, who are protected by the power of God through faith for a salvation ready to be revealed in the last time.**
> (1 Peter 1:3-5 NASB)

Peter says that "the inheritance" which was "reserved in heaven" for them, was the "salvation" that was "ready to be revealed" in the last time. Contextually this makes sense, and stands alone. However, when we consider that the terms "imperishable, undefiled, and reserved in heaven" (which describe the inheritance) all belonged to the New Covenant world and were therefore at that time "unrevealed", it follows logically that the salvation that was "ready to be revealed" (in the natural) was the inheritance which was reserved in heaven (the spiritual).

Also, it was through "hope" that they would receive their inheritance (v.3-4) and through "faith" that that they would receive their salvation (v.5). **According to Peter, inheritance and salvation are synonymous redemptive elements.** To receive the inheritance was to receive salvation, and that salvation was their full inheritance. This truth that inheritance equals salvation is echoed and magnified through the other apostolic voices in the New Testament.

Listen to what the writer of Hebrews says.

> **Are they not all ministering spirits, sent out to render service for the sake of those who will inherit salvation?** (Hebrews 1:14 NASB)

The writer of Hebrews says plainly that salvation is the inheritance. Said another way, salvation would come through their inheritance. Also, the world "will" is from the Greek word *"mello"* and means "about to, on the point of" which is translated more accurately below.

> **Are they not all spirits of service — for ministration being sent forth because of those about to inherit salvation?** (Hebrews 1:14 YLT)

So, not only does inheritance equal salvation, but that salvation was "about to be received" when the book of Hebrews was written. Apostle Paul echoes this thought in his letter to the Romans.

> **Do this, knowing the time, that it is already the hour for you to awaken from sleep; for**

**now salvation is nearer to us than when we believed.** (Romans 13:11)

So according to the above texts, the inheritance was their salvation (atonement), which had not been fully received as late as AD63, but was about to be, it was near. But here is the catch, their salvation was to be received at the coming (Parousia) of the Lord.

**So also Christ died once for all time as a sacrifice to take away the sins of many people. He will come again, not to deal with our sins, but to bring salvation to all who are eagerly waiting for him.** (Hebrews 9:28 NLT)

Here in syllogistic form, is the implication of the inheritance being received through covenantal transition in the first century.

**The inheritance was received through the first century covenantal transition in AD 70. (Galatians 3-4, see chapter 2)**

**The inheritance is the salvation that was near, and about to be revealed in the first century.**
**(1 Peter 1, Hebrews 9:28, Romans 13:11, see above)**

**Therefore, their salvation-inheritance was received through the first century covenantal transition in AD 70.**

But, Christ was to bring their salvation at His "coming", when he appeared the "second time". (Hebrews 9)

Therefore:

> **The New Covenant was established and covenantal transition was consummated in AD 70 when Christ "appeared the second time" with their salvation - inheritance.**

The implication is that if the inheritance was received through covenantal transition in AD 70, then so was their salvation at the coming of the Lord. This means that the Lord has returned.

There is one more powerful point that we should make which validates and cements this argument as truth. Peter says that their salvation was ready to be revealed in the "last time".

> **Who are protected by the power of God through faith for a salvation ready to be revealed in the last time.** (1 Peter 1:5)

However, a few verses later Peter tells us by divine inspiration that he was living in those "last times".

**For He was foreknown before the foundation of the world, but has appeared in these last times for the sake of you.** (1 Peter 1:20)

Then we have the writer of Hebrews saying that salvation was "about to be" inherited.

**Are they not all spirits of service — for ministration being sent forth because of those about to inherit salvation?** (Hebrews 1:14 YLT)

> So, according to these inspired apostolic voices, their salvation was "ready" and "about to be" inherited (received) in those last times. In other words, their salvation was at that time imminent, it was "at hand".

In light of this, consider the following:

The scriptures teach that the consummative salvation-inheritance was near/at hand in the first century.

But, that salvation would come at the coming of the Lord

Therefore, the coming of the Lord was near/at hand in the first century.

If this argument is to withstand the test of scripture, then we should expect to find the New Testament writers, and Jesus, saying this very thing - that the coming of the Lord was near/at hand in their days. This is exactly the apostolic testimony that we do find in the pages of the New Testament.

> **For you have need of endurance, so that when you have done the will of God, you may receive what was promised. For yet in a very little while, he who is coming will come, and will not delay.** (Hebrews 10:36-37)

> **Therefore, be patient, brethren, until the coming of the Lord. The farmer waits for the precious produce of the soil, being patient about it, until it gets the early and late rains. You too be patient; strengthen your hearts, for the coming (Parousia) of the Lord is near. Do not complain, brethren, against one another, so that you yourselves may not be judged; behold, the Judge is standing right at the door.**
> (James 5:7-9)

> **As He was sitting on the Mount of Olives, the disciples came to Him privately, saying, "Tell us, when will these things happen, and what will be the sign of Your coming, (Parousia) and of the end of the age?"… And then the sign of the**

Son of Man will appear in the sky, and then all the tribes of the earth will mourn, and they will see the Son of man, coming on the clouds of the sky with power and great glory…. "Truly I say to you, this generation will not pass away until all these things take place. (Mathew 24:3,30,34)

Blessed is he who reads and those who hear the words of the prophecy, and heed the things which are written in it; for the time is near… And he said to me, "Do not seal up the words of the prophecy of this book, for the time is near… Behold, I am coming quickly, and My reward is with Me, to render to every man according to what he has done… He who testifies to these things says, "Yes, I am coming quickly." Amen. Come, Lord Jesus. (Revelation 1:3, 22:10,12,20)

---

Not only does scripture teach that Israel's consummative salvation-inheritance was near/at hand in the first century. It also teaches that the coming (Parousia) of the Lord, which would bring that salvation - inheritance was likewise near/at hand in the first century.

---

So, if the popular opinion of "orthodox Christianity" that the Lord has not yet returned is true, then the body of Christ (True Israel) has not yet received salvation nor the inheritance of Abraham, and the work of atonement and redemption remain unfulfilled and incomplete. I fully reject this view as unbiblical and Christ dishonoring, yet I mean no disrespect to the individuals who hold to this paradigm in ignorance.

Instead, I submit the following conclusion for your consideration:

The consummative salvation of Israel was received as their inheritance in AD 70 at the establishment of the New Covenant, through the process of covenantal transition. Biblically, the salvation of Israel was to be received at the coming (Parousia) of the Lord. Therefore, the coming (Parousia) of the Lord took place in AD 70 which brought the promised salvation - inheritance to the remnant of Israel through the establishment of the New Covenant, and consummated the process of covenantal transition.

# THE IMPLICATIONS OF THE KINGDOM THROUGH COVENANTAL TRANSITION

What is the significance of the fact that the Kingdom of God was received in the first century through covenantal transition, and what is the implication for us today? As we shall demonstrate below, since the Messianic Kingdom was received through covenantal transition in the first century, this means that the "second coming" (Parousia) of the Lord was also a first century event which brought national restoration to Israel in Christ. Both Old and New Testaments connect the concepts of "Kingdom and Coming" together, that is, to occur at the same time.

> **In other words, the Kingdom could only come and be received in its fullness at the coming of the King.**

We will demonstrate clearly that the coming of the kingdom cannot be separated from the coming of the King.

**I kept looking in the night visions, and behold, with the clouds of heaven one like a Son of Man was coming, and He came up to the Ancient of Days and was presented before Him. And to Him was given dominion, glory and a kingdom, that all the peoples, nations and men of every language might serve Him. His dominion is an everlasting dominion which will not pass away; and His kingdom is one which will not be destroyed.... But the saints of the Most High shall take the kingdom, and possess the kingdom forever, even for ever and ever.... I kept looking, and that horn was waging war**

**with the saints and overpowering them, until the Ancient of days came, and judgment was given to the saints of the Most High; and the time came that the saints possessed the kingdom…. And the kingdom and dominion, and the greatness of the kingdom under the whole heaven, shall be given to the people of the saints of the Most High, whose kingdom is an everlasting kingdom, and all dominions shall serve and obey him.** (Dan.7:13-27)

As a side note, it should be noticed that Daniel places the receiving of the kingdom by the "saints" at the time of the judgment of the "little horn" (v.8-10) which is when the "books were opened". This judgment is parallel to the judgment in John's Revelation and is also known as the "great white throne judgment" (Revelation 20:11-15).

Clearly, the receiving of the kingdom by the saints in Daniel 7 is not a reference to the ascension of Jesus and his inauguration as King, nor to Pentecost and the initiation of the kingdom through the giving of the Holy Spirit. Rather, **Daniel 7 prophesied the time when the people of God would receive the consummated and fully established Messianic Kingdom at the coming of the Lord in power, in judgment, and in great glory.** What must not be overlooked in all this is the fact that Daniel clearly places the time of the fulfillment of his prophecy in the days of the "fourth beast", that is, in the days of the Roman empire. And, that is precisely when

the New Testament writers tell us that the time for the establishment of the kingdom as prophesied by Daniel had come.

> **Now after John had been taken into custody, Jesus came into Galilee, preaching the gospel of God, and saying, "The time is fulfilled, and the kingdom of God is at hand; repent and believe in the gospel."** (Mark 1:14-15)

There should be no doubt that Jesus' words were spoken in anticipation of the soon fulfillment of Daniel's prophecy. Notice the comparison below.

> **".... and the time came that the saints possessed the kingdom..."** (Daniel 7:22)

> **".... the time is fulfilled, and the kingdom of God is at hand"** (Mark 1:15)

The "appointed time" had come for the saints to possess the kingdom of God which Daniel said would come during the reign of Rome.

Jesus validated the words of the prophet Daniel when he said that both the coming of the kingdom and his coming in glory would occur within his own generation, in the days of the fourth beast-Rome.

> Thus, Jesus connected the coming of the kingdom with his coming (Parousia) as "same time events".

For the Son of Man is going to come in the glory of His Father with His angels, and will then repay every man according to his deeds. Truly I say to you, there are some of those who are standing here who will not taste death until they see the Son of Man coming in His kingdom."
(Mathew 16:27-28)

Luke records Jesus saying basically the same thing in the context of Jerusalem's destruction in AD 70. Thus, Luke connects the coming of the kingdom and the coming of the Lord within that first century generation, to the destruction of Jerusalem in AD 70.

As for these things which you are looking at, the days will come in which there will not be left one stone upon another which will not be torn down".... But when you see Jerusalem surrounded by armies, then recognize that her desolation is near. Then those who are in Judea must flee to the mountains, and those who are in the midst of the city must leave, and those who are in the country must not enter the city; because these are days of vengeance, so that all

**things which are written will be fulfilled... Then they will see the Son of man coming in a cloud with power and great glory... So you also, when you see these things happening, recognize that the kingdom of God is near. Truly I say to you, this generation will not pass away until all things take place.** (Luke 21:6,21-22, 27-32)

But, not only did Jesus connect the coming of the kingdom with his coming (Parousia), but so did his disciples.

**I solemnly charge you in the presence of God and of Christ Jesus, who is to judge the living and the dead, and by His appearing and His kingdom.** (1 Timothy 4:1)

**But each in his own order: Christ the first fruits, after that those who are Christ's at His coming, then comes the end, when He hands over the kingdom to the God and Father, when He has abolished all rule and all authority and power.** (1 Corinthians 15:23-24)

Let's look at one more text which will establish our position beyond doubt.

**Listen to another parable. There was a landowner who planted a vineyard and put a**

wall around it and dug a wine press in it and built a tower, and rented it out to vine-growers and went on a journey.... Therefore, when the owner of the vineyard comes, what will he do to those vine-growers?" They said to Him, "He will bring those wretches to a wretched end, and will rent out the vineyard to other vine-growers who will pay him the proceeds at the proper seasons." Jesus said to them, "Did you never read in the Scriptures, "The stone which the builders rejected, this became the chief corner stone, this came about from the Lord and it is marvelous in our eyes." Therefore, I say to you the kingdom of God will be taken away from you and given to a people, producing the fruit of it.... When the chief priests and the Pharisees heard His parables, they understood that He was speaking about them. (Mathew 21:33-45)**

Notice that the landowner went on a "journey," but was to return (come again). At his coming (return), he would bring to an end those who had murdered his servants and His Son by taking away from them the kingdom of God, and giving that kingdom to another people. Based on the above texts we have proven that:

1. The appointed time for the kingdom to be established as prophesied in Daniel had come.
   (Daniel 2,7 Mark 1:14- 15)

2. The coming of the kingdom is connected to the coming of the King (the Parousia of Christ), they are same-time-events. (Mathew 16:27-28)

3. Both the coming of the kingdom and the coming of the Lord were to occur within the first century generation, and were connected to the destruction of Jerusalem in AD 70. (Luke 21, Mathew 24, Revelation 11)

4. The coming of the Lord in the destruction of Jerusalem in AD 70 to take vengeance on those who had killed him and his servants, was the time when the kingdom of God would be taken from Old Covenant Israel and given to another people. The body of Christ - New Covenant Israel, would receive the restored and transformed Kingdom of God at the coming of the Lord in AD 70.

If "orthodox Christianity" is true, that the consummative Messianic Kingdom has not yet been established, then the Old Covenant kingdom under Torah still remains covenantally valid, and that "shakable" kingdom still belongs to Old Covenant Israel - the natural (flesh) seed of Abraham.

Furthermore, if the Messianic kingdom has not been established, then the "unshakable" New Covenant has not been established either, and all the redemptive elements of the New Covenant have yet to be fully applied to those in Christ – the spiritual Seed of Abraham. (Galatians 4, Hebrews 12)

Once again, I fully reject any paradigm which posits the redemptive work of Jesus Christ as yet unfulfilled.

Instead, I submit the following for your consideration:

True Israel (the spiritual body of Christ) has received the Kingdom through the first century covenantal transition.

The Old Covenant form of that Kingdom was "taken" from ethnic Israel, transformed in Christ, and given to God's New-Israel in its spiritual New Covenant form.

Through the coming of the King in glory in AD 70, He has consummated both kingdom and covenantal transition.

# THE IMPLICATIONS OF THE IMAGE OF GOD THROUGH COVENANTAL TRANSITION

Ask yourself, what is the significance in the fact that the image of God was restored to man in the first century through covenantal transition, and what is the implication for us today?

As we will demonstrate below, since the image of God has been restored to man through covenantal transition, then the resurrection has taken place, the consummation has come. We will prove this to be true by demonstrating that the image of the resurrected-man is the same image as the New Covenant-man.

As a brief review, we have already established from 2 Corinthians 3 that man was being restored to the image of God through the first century covenantal transition.

> **But we all, with unveiled face, beholding as in a mirror the glory of the Lord, are being transformed into the same image (*eikon* -D.D.) from glory to glory, just as from the Lord, the Spirit.** (2 Corinthians 3:18)

> **However, because the first century covenantal transition is now complete, this demands that man's transformation into the image of God is likewise complete.**

Therefore, man (through Israel) has been restored to the image of God in the New Covenant, through covenantal transition. With that thought in our minds, let's move on.

The Greek word for image in 2 Corinthians 3 is *"eikon"*, which means "image, figure, likeness, representation". Now, although this word is used over 20 times in the New Testament, what's very interesting is that it is used in two other texts to refer to the "image" of man in the consummative resurrected state. In other words, **in the following two texts, *"eikon"* refers to man's restoration to the image of God through the final resurrection.**

> **For I reckon that the sufferings of the present time are not worthy to be compared with the glory about to be revealed in us…. And not only this, but also we ourselves, having the first fruits of the Spirit, even we ourselves groan within ourselves, waiting eagerly for our adoption as sons, the redemption of our body…. For those whom He foreknew, He also predestined to become conformed to the image (*eikon* -D.D.) of His Son, so that He would be the firstborn among many brethren.** (Romans 8:18-29)

Notice in the above text that being conformed to the "image of the Son" would make them "brethren" of Jesus. But according to the text, to become a brother of Jesus they would need to be "adopted as sons".

Logically this makes sense, one cannot be a "brethren of the Son" without also being a "son" himself. However, that son-ship would only come through "the adoption" - the resurrection (v.23).

> This means that when they were adopted as sons they would be "conformed to the image of the Son". Said another way, resurrection would restore them to the image of the Son through adoption.

So also it is written, "The first man, Adam, became a living soul." The last Adam *became* a life-giving spirit... The first man is from the earth, earthy; the second man is from heaven. As is the earthy, so also are those who are earthy; and as is the heavenly, so also are those who are heavenly. Just as we have borne the image (*eikon* -D.D.) of the earthy, we will also bear the image (*eikon* -D.D.) of the heavenly... Behold, I tell you a mystery; we will not all sleep, but we will all be changed, in a moment, in the twinkling of an eye, at the last trumpet; for the trumpet will sound, and the dead will be raised imperishable, and we will be changed.
(1 Corinthians 15:45-52)

Notice in this text that their "image" would be changed from the image of Adam into the image of Christ at the resurrection. Through resurrection, they would bear the image of "the heavenly".

Here is what these texts teach.

Their "transformation" into the **image (*eikon*)** of Christ would be complete at the establishment (consummation) of the New Covenant in AD 70, when "covenantal transition" was complete. (2 Corinthians 3:11-18, Hebrews 10:9)

Their "conformation" into the **image (*eikon*)** of Christ (the image of the Son) would be complete at the adoption as sons, the redemption of the body - the resurrection.
(Romans 8:23-29)

Their "change" into the **image (*eikon*)** of Christ (the image of the heavenly) would be complete at the resurrection.
(1 Corinthians 15:49)

Based on the statements above, we present the following:

The image of God was restored to man through the covenantal transition which consummated in AD 70, and the establishment of the New Covenant.

But, the image of God would be restored to man at the final resurrection.

The image of God was restored to man at the final resurrection which took place in AD 70 as the consummation of the covenantal transition, and the establishment of the New Covenant.

The chart on the next page provides powerful evidence that **all three texts refer to the same "change" into the same "image" which 2 Corinthians 3 clearly places in the first century, through the process of covenantal transition.**

| 2 Corinthians 3 | Romans 8 | 1 Corinthians 15 |
|---|---|---|
| From glory to glory (2 Corinthians 3:18) | Glory about to be revealed (Romans 8:18) | Glory of the heavenly, glory of the earthy (1 Corinthians 15:40) |
| Transformed into the image (2 Corinthians 3:18) | Conformed to the image (Romans 8:29 | Changed into the image (1 Corinthians 15:49, 52) |
| The image of the Lord (2 Corinthians 3:18) | The image of the Son (Romans 8:29) | The image of the earthy (1 Corinthians 15:49) |
| Having such a hope (2 Corinthians 3:12) | Saved by hope (Romans 8:24) | Hoped in Christ (1 Corinthians 15:19) |
| Veil remains un-lifted (2 Corinthians 3:14) | Revealing of the sons of God (Romans 8:19) | Mortal will have put on immortality (1 Corinthians 15:48) |
| The ministration of condemnation (2 Corinthians 3:9) | Made subject to vanity (Romans 8:20) | The power of sin is the law (1 Corinthians 15:56) |
| There is liberty (2 Corinthians 3:17) | Delivered into glorious liberty (Romans 8:21) | Death is swallowed up in victory (1 Corinthians 15:54) |
| What had glory, in this case has no glory (2 Corinthians 3:10) | Not worthy to be compared with the glory (Romans 8:18) | Sown in dishonor, raised in glory (1 Corinthians 15:43) |
| Present sufferings (2 Corinthians 4:16) | Sufferings of this present time (Romans 8:18) | In danger every hour, I die daily (1 Corinthians 15:30-31) |

While 2 Corinthians 3 emphasizes the "process" of the change, Romans 8 and 1 Corinthians 15 emphasize the "consummation" of that process. Look at it like this.

In 2 Corinthians 3 they were *being* (present active indicative) **"transformed"** (*metamorphoo*) **into the image** (*eikon*) of Christ through covenantal transition.

In Romans 8 they would be **"conformed"** (*symmorphos*) **into the image (eikon)** of Christ at the adoption.

In 1 Corinthians 15 they would be **"changed"** (*allasso*) **into the image** (*eikon*) of Christ at the resurrection.

> **This means that the final resurrection - change (*allasso*) was the consummation of the then ongoing transformation (*metamorphoo*) process of covenantal transition, which when completed, "conformed" (*symmorphos*) them to the image of Christ.**

Now think about this carefully. If the above argument is not true (as the majority of modern Christianity would insist), then we are forced to say that man will be restored to the image of Christ, at two different times in history. **The first time being in AD 70,** when man was restored to the image of Christ in the first century, through covenantal transition. But **the second time being sometime in the future,** when man will bear the image of Christ through an apparent future bodily resurrection. And worst of all, this conclusion implies that those in Christ do not presently bear the image of Christ, at least not the "real image". This seems to me an untenable and indefensible position.

> **To say that the image of God was restored to man in and through the New Covenant, but then insist that we still bear the "image of the earthy" and are awaiting a future resurrection to bear the "image of the heavenly", is nonsensical.**

However, if scripture teaches only one restoration of man to the image of God at only one time period in history, then the syllogistic argument from above must be true. Here it is again:

The image of God was restored to man through covenantal transition which consummated in AD 70 with the establishment of the New Covenant.

But, the image of God would be restored to man at the final resurrection.

Therefore, the image of God was restored to man at the final resurrection which took place in AD 70 as the consummation of covenantal transition, and the establishment of the New Covenant.

Unless it can be proven that 1 Corinthians 15 and Romans 8 speak of a different image of Christ than 2 Corinthians 3, then our position stands. **The resurrection took place in AD 70 at the consummation of covenantal transition, which restored the** image of God to man and established the New Covenant.

# CONCLUSION

Based on the ground we have covered in this book, these are our conclusions:

In chapter one we established that **between AD30 and AD 70 both Old and New Covenants were in transition.**

In chapter two we established that **Israel's inheritance was received through Covenantal Transition in AD 70.**

In chapter three we established that **the Messianic Kingdom was received through Covenantal Transition in AD 70.**

In chapter four we established that **man was restored to the image of God through Covenantal Transition in AD 70.**

In chapter five we explored the implications of the truths established in chapters two through four, which are:

The inheritance was the salvation of Israel which was to come at the coming (Parousia) of the Lord. But, since the inheritance was received through covenantal transition in AD 70, this means that **the Lord returned and consummated Israel's salvation-inheritance in AD 70.**

The Messianic Kingdom was to come (be established) and be received by the saints at the coming of the Lord. But, since the kingdom was received through covenantal transition in AD 70, this means that **the Lord returned to establish his kingdom which he gave to his servants as their inheritance in AD 70.**

The image of God was to be restored to man at the final resurrection. But, since the image of God was restored to man through covenantal transition in AD 70, this means that **the resurrection took place through covenantal transition in AD 70.**

Finally, since the covenants were in fact in transition in the first century, this demands that the consummative-redemptive elements of those covenants were likewise in transition at the same time. Throughout this work we have looked at three of those redemptive elements; the inheritance, the kingdom, and the image of God. These redemptive elements were therefore received by Israel through covenantal transition when the Old Covenant, after serving its prophetic purpose, was fully accomplished and passed away thus revealing the New.

Since AD 70, the consummative-redemptive elements of the New Covenant have been received, the consummation has come! Because Israel has been restored and has received all her promises in the body of Christ, those of us now in Christ, presently partake of His finished work.

With all traditions and dogmas laid aside, the consistent testimony of the scriptures declares to us, that the consummation has come through the transition between two covenants.

Search it, study it, ponder it, fight this if you must. But if you cannot refute it, then embrace it, and in your own time join us and help us to restore the glorious truth of....

## The Finished Work of Jesus Christ through The Transition Between Two Covenants.

Made in the USA
Lexington, KY
25 May 2018